Praise for *Warrior Sisters*

In this family memoir readers will be captured by the candidness and vulnerability of authors, Kelly and Karen, sisters raised in an abusive alcoholic family. Their life stories reflect familial pain, consequences of different ways of coping, and the search for ways to emotionally and physically survive. It's a beautiful memoir that aptly describes the insidiousness of addiction, the potential and promises that are fulfilled in recovery, and the power of love. Truly inspirational!

— ***Claudia Black,*** *PhD, author of Unspoken Legacy and*
It Will Never Happen to Me

ↄ

Kelly and Karen have pulled off a page turner from beginning to end. Each of their stories is raw and insightful and has an "everyman" element to it. I found myself walking away from each chapter with the sense that I'd been watching my own life while reading about theirs. *Warrior Sisters* brilliantly describes the feelings and images of their struggles with addiction. It is for anyone who has eyes to see and ears to hear. *Warrior Sisters* beautifully delves deeply into the painful despair of addiction and then turns the corner toward relief and healing. The tone changes dramatically toward the experience of peace, joy, and hope. This is a great book to share with anyone. It begs for more stories to be told. And just maybe the next story is yours?

— ***Tim Timmons,*** *author Anyone Anonymous*

ↄ

This story of heartbreak and healing, addiction and broken expectations that only God almighty could redeem ranks as one of the most moving stories of God triumphing over evil that I have seen in my two decades of experience. "And they have conquered him by the blood of the Lamb and by the word of their testimony, for they loved not their lives even unto death" (Revelation 12:11 ESV). *Warrior Sisters* is a beautiful human interest story and a must-read life redeeming message of hope.

— **Mike Modica,** *pastor of First Assembly DeLand Church and DeLand police chaplain*

❧

Alcoholism, drug addiction, domestic violence, and co-dependency are the weeds in the garden of life. This is a compelling story of a journey that explains how the weeds take root and destroy the garden. Family, faith, and professionals can help restore sanity and sunshine. *Warrior Sisters* made me appreciate the small blessings of life. Triumphant and courageous!

— **Patty Evans,** *CMO, Meadows Behavioral Healthcare*

❧

Warrior Sisters is an inspiring and honest true story of two sisters and the visible and hidden lies of addiction. An incredibly vulnerable and moving story of recovery that grabs you from the start with simplicity and hopefulness and doesn't let go. I cried, I laughed, and when I read the last word, I was speechless—what a story. I couldn't put the book down. A must read for anyone who is feeling stuck and hopeless. Truly heart-warming!

— **Karen Eusebio,** *MS life coach*

છ૭

Warrior Sisters is an engrossing story of two sisters and their very different paths to addiction, the dangerous relationships addition leads to, and the common ways the disease destroys anyone attempting to love the addict. It will open your eyes to the way the disease lulls its victims with denial and a dark and blurry existence. It is horrifying the way the disease stalks some family members and spares others. Read this book to realize how fragile we all are, to attempt to understand anyone around you who seems to have succumbed, and to learn how holding secrets and allowing lies to go unchallenged is what provides fertile ground for the disease of addiction.

— **Fran Gallaher,**
Intuitive life coach, writer, and speaker

છ૭

WARRIOR
SISTERS

FOR:
Kenzie
With gratitude,
Karen & Kelly

WARRIOR SISTERS

One was a drunk, the other a junkie.
To help each other, they had to
save themselves first.

Kelly Ryan, LMFT & Karen Burd

ILLUMIFY
MEDIA.COM

WARRIOR SISTERS

Scripture quotations are taken from the New King James Version®. Copyright © 1982 by Thomas Nelson. Used by permission. All rights reserved.

The views and opinions expressed in this book are those of the author and do not necessarily reflect the official policy or position of Illumify Media Global.

Published by
Illumify Media Global
www.IllumifyMedia.com
"Let's bring your book to life!"

Library of Congress Control Number: 2021915790

Paperback ISBN: 978-1-955043-46-5
eBook ISBN: 978-1-955043-47-2

Typeset by Art Innovations (http://artinnovations.in/)
Cover design by Debbie Lewis

Printed in the United States of America

Dedication

For our mother, Rosemarie Hinkle, our angel, champion, and hero.
She was and is the foundation of our family.
We love you, honor you, and thank you.

Contents

Introduction

This is a true story, written by two sisters who reveal their family dysfunction, trauma, alcoholism, addiction, and eventually their recovery. Two sisters with distinct personalities and unique life experiences but both with an innate ability to persevere, no matter what the circumstances.

Little did we know that the unresolved trauma from our childhood and the demands of daily living would lead us to alcoholism and addiction. We spent years seeking relief by anesthetizing ourselves. The level of complete destruction and annihilation our disease had on our family was indescribable. Yet somehow, through the love of our mother, we maintained an impenetrable bond.

Our experiences have been threads in a tapestry that have woven our lives together forever. Our greatest desire is that this story touches someone, anyone, who is looking for change. It is always darkest before the dawn. Based on our experiences, we believe this to be a universal truth. There is always hope and healing for those who seek it.

Our stories are reflected and interwoven into each chapter, presenting to the reader a dual memoir and a family chronicle.

You'll find that we have identified which sister is speaking as each chapter begins.

While we have lived very different lives, our stories have a common theme: the unbreakable bond between two sisters and their fight for freedom.

Meet Kelly

I'm a licensed marriage and family therapist. My undergraduate degree is in special education, which led me to teaching students labeled as emotionally disturbed and the learning disabled. These were the labels commonly used in the early 1980s. I have spent more than thirty-five years in the field of education, mental health, substance abuse treatment, and recovery. My professional life has been dedicated to assisting families with troubled children. My mission is to help families break multigenerational patterns that inhibit them from experiencing joy in the here and now.

I had a high bottom. In other words, I didn't need to allow addiction to destroy everything in my life before I admitted that I had a problem and asked for help. I could see where drug addiction and alcoholism had taken my father and sister and did not want to experience the same pain, consequences, and decline they did. I spent a good portion of my adult life trying to control my drinking and learning to manage the unmanageable. Addiction is insidious. In fact, my father died in May 2019 at age seventy-six from cirrhosis of the liver and alcoholism. He died isolated, alone, and estranged from his children.

Meet Karen

For many years I was stubborn and selfish. Let's just say I lived life on *my* terms and was unwilling to compromise. Of course, life has a way of getting through to even the most stubborn of us. Eventually, my life did just that.

I destroyed the relationships that were the most precious things in the world to me: my relationship with my three sisters, my mother, my stepfather, and my boyfriend. I was a liar. I no longer knew the truth because I lied to myself so often that I could not determine the difference between the truth and a lie. In fact, at one point in my recovery, I had to check and ask myself if my thoughts were real. Sometimes I ran my ideas by others to determine if what I was thinking had any validity.

Navigating life became nearly impossible for me because my mind had become sick and delusional. I had damaged my brain with an enormous variety of substances in massive amounts, and it took a while for my brain to recover.

Amazingly, I believe my recovery includes the full restoration of my mind, body, and soul.

KELLY SPEAKS

A sad truth is alcoholics and/or addicts may experience more than one bottom. Moments that take them down so low no one believed it was not dark and deep enough to make them turn around and admit they have a problem. You will see that our alcoholism presented differently, progressed differently, and resolved differently.

Karen drank alcoholically from her first drink at age fourteen. My disease was slow and progressive over many years. We will be sharing with you more about the progression of the disease in each of us, as well as our recoveries.

I emerged from alcoholism and got sober sooner than Karen. Therefore, my voice will provide the perspective of what was both sane and insane in my story and Karen's story. Because of my education and experience, my voice will be more clinical. Karen's voice reflects street life, the voice of a junkie who was immersed in drug addiction for a long, long time. Her disease would take her to death's door before she was willing to accept the wisdom of those who offered a solution and recovery.

Karen was the firstborn. She always needed to experience things firsthand. She would not listen to advice, seek support, or accept mentorship. I was the third born out of four children. I'm sure I benefited from witnessing the mistakes of my older sisters. I didn't need to experience things firsthand. I could observe, evaluate, and had the ability to predict specific outcomes. I sought out support and mentorship from adults, and I believe this shaped me. Somehow, as a child, I knew that education was my "way out" of a chaotic and abusive childhood.

Families are our greatest teachers, and we, like you, had many lessons. We hope you can identify with our two different journeys and range of life experiences of rebellion, redemption, and recovery.

The book is about the remarkable journeys of two ordinary drunks who eventually became people capable of extraordinary contributions and today dedicate their lives to passing on the message of recovery. We have done so for no other reason than to assist others suffering from the disease of addiction. In fact, we are *compelled* to pass on the message of recovery as an attempt to pay forward the gifts we received from those who traveled before us.

1

The Beginning of the End

KAREN'S STORY

It is odd to me that I can recall these memories without feeling the horrendous hopelessness that permeated this time in my life. I was fifty-two years old, smoking crack cocaine, hanging out with street criminals, drinking, and stem-fast skinny. I hadn't worked in ten years but had money from a retirement plan and, therefore, felt financially secure. I owned a home that had turned into a known drug house and because there are always people around when you have money to pay for the party, I never worried. I spent my time and money on the fastest downhill track in life.

I believed in nothing at this point in my life, certainly not in God or myself. As a matter of fact, there was nothing of me left. Any personality or joy I'd once had in life was eaten by an ugly monster created from my lifelong abuse of drugs and alcohol. The real me did not exist anymore. I was like one of the walking dead.

My "friends" were local dope boys, prostitutes, and other crackheads. I sincerely cared about most of these people.

Their spirits were as beautiful as anyone else's, and most had dreams of a decent life. But mental illness, shattered childhoods, poverty, generational lifestyles, and plain old bad choices had interrupted those dreams, and now addiction ruled our lives every breathing moment. It ruled every decision or choice there was to make, especially toward the end near my rock bottom.

Gradually, I began living in a state of paranoia. I believed there was a vast conspiracy with everyone in town out to kill me and take over my life. My paranoia and suspicion got so bad I drove to the FBI offices in Jacksonville, Florida, to see an agent and beg them to check out my theories.

I was also convinced the air in my home was making me ill. I could not breathe when I was inside unless all doors and windows were open. Even then, I could only be inside for about ten minutes.

I took samples of dirt from my backyard, water from the spigots, and hair from my head. I sent them to labs to see what was poisoning me. Something had to be very wrong for me to be acting like I was.

Before long, I started living in a hotel sixty miles from my house and driving home daily to get my dope supply. Part of me knew I was living in crazy town. I couldn't distinguish between a rational thought or a distorted, psychotic one. One day, a true friend stopped by my home to check on me. When I shared my fears with him, he suggested that I put the crack pipe down and quit getting high for a while.

"It can't be the crack," I said, laughing and gesturing with the pipe I was holding. "I always do this, and I've never had thoughts like these before."

I did not understand cocaine psychosis at the time, but it wouldn't have mattered one bit if I had. The idea of not using drugs never even occurred to me. I could not quit anyway. I'd tried before and couldn't handle failing one more time.

Things were going downhill fast.

Eventually, my life became unlivable. Picture this: I had cut all the tv, stereo, and phone wires in my home so no one could watch me or hear my thoughts. Most of my furniture was on the front lawn because I believed I had contaminated it. Every person in my life had fled because they could not watch my destruction any longer. I was even too much for the other crackheads to deal with.

And then I hit my final bottom.

It began as a typical day for me. I had met up with one of my dealers and was sitting in his car while he weighed my dope. I had known him for maybe six months and had grown fond of him. In my eyes, he was just a regular guy who happened to sell drugs—good drugs. No bougie for me. Only the good stuff.

I noticed there was a tiny New Testament in his car.

By this time, I had been to jail a few times and exposed to countless Alcoholics Anonymous (AA) meetings. While I had a basic belief that God existed, I couldn't understand why a supposedly loving Father would want any of His children to experience a life of using and drug deals.

Seeing that small book, I had a mind-blowing epiphany. I realized, for the first time ever, that I did not *have* to buy and use drugs. Why this thought had never crossed my mind before, I do not know.

Moments later, I burst into uncontrollable sobs.

My dealer must have been freaked because one minute he was doing a typical drug deal, and the next minute he was trying to comfort me.

"What's wrong?" he asked, looking confused and somewhat scared.

I sobbed harder.

"It's okay," he said. "You don't have to buy this."

Hearing that, I felt sorry for him. Who would have thought that his duties as a drug dealer would include counseling me!

As I calmed down, I remember feeling like I didn't want to live like this any longer. I also knew it did not matter because I did not know how to live any other way.

When I got home and hit the pipe, the word *relief* came out of my mouth. That is all I had ever been trying to find: relief. Relief from my thoughts, my failures, my darkness, my empty soul, and from life in general. I'd always felt ill-equipped to deal with this world.

One night—I don't remember if it was a few hours later, a week later, or a month later—I fell to my knees in my empty living room in the dark. I felt so confused. I made noises I never knew were in me—a combination of screams, sobs, death wishes, and fear.

After some time of being curled up in a ball on the floor, I had a clear thought that had not occurred to me before in a sincere way. The thought was to pray. I know the thought did not come from me because I had written off prayer many years before, considering it the way of simple-minded people with no self-sufficiency or guts.

"God," I said aloud, "if You are real, either fix me or kill me."

Truthfully, I didn't care what choice He made. Death sounded better because it would be easier, instant, and permanent. Living sounded way too hard.

I asked God to make that choice for me—with one caveat. If He decided I should live, He was going to have to do it all. I had no idea where to start, nor did I have the energy. In an instant moment of clarity, I realized I never learned how to live sober. I realized I had no idea how to live a successful life, or maybe I should say a "happy" life.

I fell asleep that night in a strangely peaceful state.

The year was 2013.

KELLY SPEAKS

During this period of time, I had many conversations with Karen while she was in a drug-induced psychosis. For both of us, getting sober was not a single moment or one effective intervention. I want to make that clear to our readers; it took many tries and many small moments of insights before we got sober. Many of those insights were provided by the people around us. Some were mired in addiction just as we were; others, especially for me, were mentors or part of my professional life.

Alcoholism and drug addiction do not discriminate. All ages, races, cultures, and socio-economic levels are represented. Society still has preconceived notions about what drunks today look like. Society may envision them begging for money on a freeway exit, see them pushing a shopping cart with their belongings stacked high, or observe a bum living under a bridge.

While these stereotypes exist, most alcoholics and addicts today are your doctor, your neighbor, your lawyer, your boss, your kids' teachers, and other average people you don't picture as being afflicted. We are well-respected members of the community and blend in easily with daily routines.

KELLY'S STORY

I am a "high bottom" drunk. I never got a DUI or lost a job, a home, or my husband. As a matter of fact, I was at the top of my career. I stayed in denial because I could look at my sister Karen, along with many of my alcoholic friends, and say, "I'm not as bad as they are."

I was not, but in the end, none of that mattered.

What mattered was that I was lost and in conflict about my drinking, not to mention very unhappy. I was like every other active alcoholic with a "hole in their soul." I isolated, which enabled me to drink alone and drink daily.

I would drink to celebrate.

I would drink to take the edge off.

I would drink after a tennis match.

I would drink after a workout.

I would drink when I was angry.

I would drink alone in hotel bars and hotel rooms.

In addition to all that drinking, wining and dining customers was part of my job description. Drinking was part of the corporate culture, and there was not a day that went by when I could not find a valid reason to drink!

Almost every morning I would wake up hungover with cotton-mouth, head pounding, eyes swollen, and my nose bright red. I'd immediately look to see if my husband was still beside me. If I had been mean, Bob would be up and gone to work before I woke up. I had to look because I could never remember. Had I been nasty to my husband? Had we fought? Had I said something I shouldn't have?

And every morning I would say to myself, *Why did I drink like this again? I am not drinking today!*

By noon, I would be so obsessed with feeling anxious and thinking about not drinking that I knew by four or five in the afternoon, I would be uncorking another bottle of wine.

I knew the jig was up when Bob asked to speak to me. With tears in his eyes, he told me he had a plan to leave me. He'd had enough of my destructive lifestyle, and it was damaging him too.

He sat me down and, with great care and concern, stated that he was no longer willing to be part of my drinking problem. My drinking was interfering with our relationship to such an extent that if he stayed in our marriage, he would be enabling me to continue to drink myself to death.

We owned a rental property, and the tenant had just moved out, so it was perfect timing. Bob explained that he would move into the condo while he decided what his future would be.

After fifteen years of marriage, my worst fears were coming to fruition. My husband was going to leave me. Of course, I don't know why this came as a surprise. I had spent the last fifteen years of our marriage pushing him away and manifesting my worst fear: abandonment. I truly felt I was not worthy of love. This was my self-fulfilling prophecy, and I orchestrated every bit of it. The most significant male role model I had was my father. My perception was that all men cheated, lied, abused, and eventually got bored and moved on.

And yet, now that my worst fear was coming true, I realized it was much different than I had imagined. I realized that Bob's plan to move out was actually the most selfless display of love anyone had ever shown me.

Bob loved me enough to leave me in order to help me. He did not shame me, blame me, or even threaten me. He calmly set his boundary and had a solid plan. In fact, he addressed the matter with such sincerity, love, and concern that I could not be angry.

For years, Bob and I had fought over my drinking. Oh, I would acquiesce for a temporary period. I would stop drinking for a week, sometimes a whole month, to show him I was serious about quitting. I went into therapy. I saw a psychiatrist, who prescribed antidepressants. All the while, I was lying to professionals and adamantly denying that I had a drinking problem.

This is particularly funny and ironic to me because I am a licensed marriage, and family therapist. How crazy is it to spend money on therapy sessions and lie?

It wasn't purposeful at the time; I *did* want to get help and feel better. But even though I would have moments of clarity, my minimization and denial would always kick in.

Over the years, I had tried a long list of ways to quit drinking. If you talk to any person in recovery, the themes are familiar. Here are some examples: I would limit the amount of alcohol I drank and try to do an excellent job of controlling my drinking. I would only drink after 5:00 p.m. I would not drink alone. I would stick to beer and wine and give up hard liquor. I would only drink on weekends. I would have short periods of abstinence to prove that I could give up alcohol anytime I wanted.

I broke these commitments to myself and to Bob over and over. I tried acupuncture, where they place needles in your ears to decrease cravings for alcohol. I tried hypnosis. I practiced yoga. I exercised regularly. I also attended many twelve-step meeting options: Al-Anon, Alcoholics Anonymous, and Adult Children of Alcoholics. I participated in multiple intensive workshops to resolve childhood trauma. One of the most illogical things I did was to request a prescription for Antabuse from the addiction psychiatrist I saw in therapy.

That's right, I asked for it. Myself.

Antabuse is typically mandated by the courts as an intervention for chronic alcoholics who have repeated DUIs or multiple arrests. If you are taking Antabuse and consume alcohol, you experience really unpleasant side effects, including flushing, sweating, or severe vomiting.

Antabuse is closely monitored by the courts and used for chronic alcoholics as an intervention. Typically, you must show up in person to have someone monitor and confirm you took the dosage prescribed.

So, what did I do? I learned how it worked and how long it stayed in my system so I could manipulate my use. For example, one time Bob and I went to Las Vegas, and I stopped taking Antabuse seventy-two hours before the trip to ensure that I would not throw up or get sick when I drank.

In hindsight, this was genuinely crazy behavior.

I had an honest and genuine desire to stop drinking and knew that alcohol negatively influenced my life. I had been diagnosed with chronic fatigue syndrome, fibromyalgia, and depression. I was slowly losing sight of what was important. I had broken so many promises to Bob, family members, and myself.

So when Bob told me he was leaving me, I knew it was not a threat. I knew he meant it.

While I did not get sober for Bob, it was the event that caused my bottom. Him leaving me was the final straw that broke the camel's back. It was the catalyst I needed to take a good, long look in the mirror.

I vividly remember as a teenager saying to myself that I would *never* be like my father and older sister. For years I made excuses and saw my drinking as "no big deal" compared to their blackouts, drunken rages, arrests, and car accidents. I was not anything like them.

Although my drinking was not as severe as theirs in terms of consequences or public displays, when Bob told me he was leaving me, I knew it was time for me to face the truth.

I, too, had become an alcoholic.

I, too, was lost and had a deep hole in my soul.

What used to be fun had become my worst bondage.

This realization hit me hard, and I didn't know where to turn. Fortunately, my boss was in recovery. I called her and had a complete emotional breakdown. I told her, while crying hysterically, that Bob was going to leave me because of my drinking problem.

My boss did not seem surprised and listened without judgment. At the time, we were actually working for a company that specialized in mental health and substance abuse treatment, so she helped me put a recovery plan together.

She insisted that I attend ninety AA meetings in ninety days. She suggested I try different meeting types and locations until I found a few where I felt I fit in. She encouraged me to attend women's meetings. She also agreed to be my temporary sponsor until I found a permanent one.

She ended with these words: "If you cannot do this, I'd like you to agree to go into a treatment program."

I sobbed hysterically and said I did not want to leave home. I would do anything to avoid a residential treatment intervention.

I took a medical leave of absence for an extended period from work. Interestingly, I was counseled to not disclose the truth about my alcoholism to human resources. I was told that admitting I was an alcoholic could hurt my reputation and negatively affect my chances of promotion in the future.

I was baffled by this, given that the company specialized in recovery programs and treatment interventions. In fact, the company's motto was "Help for Today, Hope for Tomorrow."

I remember thinking, *Wow, I guess it's okay to help an alcoholic, but it's not okay to be one.*

I followed the advice and took a leave of absence for "chronic fatigue syndrome." That said, I felt angry and confused. The secrecy reinforced the shame and embarrassment I felt over being an alcoholic.

Reflecting on this now, I realize the suggestion was to protect me from the stigma of being labeled an alcoholic. These stereotypes are alive and well and present in the workforce.

There's something else I've come to realize, and that is how much courage it took to admit I had a drinking problem that, on my own, I could not manage, fix, control, or stop. My efforts at sobriety had failed miserably, and it was time to ask for and accept help from others.

So, I went to ninety AA meetings in ninety days. The one I liked best was a women's meeting held at a funky metaphysical bookstore. I'll never forget the first day I walked into that gathering. I was frightened, shaking, and broken.

I found myself in a small space, very crowded and loud. The women were talking, laughing, and hugging. It was overwhelming. A woman whispered in my ear during the first meeting that I never had to take another drink. I collapsed in her arms and cried, then let her hold me for a long while.

I was so grateful that the women respected my anonymity and didn't require anything of me. I cried hysterically at meetings for eighteen months. I walked in, got hugs from the ladies, and bolted out before anyone expected me to interact. I stuttered when I introduced myself as an al-co-hol-ic. It sounded foreign coming out of my mouth.

As the women say in the program, "We will love you until you learn to love yourself." Boy, did I need a lot of loving! I didn't know how recovery or sobriety was going to work, but I had hope that maybe, just maybe, if it worked for all those women, it could work for me too.

This was in the year 2005.

2

Family Secrets

KELLY SPEAKS

It's impossible for Karen and me to talk about our path to sobriety without diving deep into the progression of our disease.

And we can't do *that* until we share a little bit about our childhood and family background. More specifically, about . . .

- the inheritance of mental illness, alcoholism, and addiction.
- the dark family secrets that led to lies, shame, abuse, and self-destruction.
- the destructive characteristics that were developed as a direct result of these multigenerational patterns.

In other words, we need to tell you a little about our family.

Karen, the oldest, was born in 1961. The second sister, Kendra, was born in 1962. I was born in 1963. Kolleen, the baby, was born in 1966. Kendra and I are known as "Irish twins" because we are eleven months apart and are the same age for one month out of every year. I get a kick out of this.

We were all born in Phillipsburg, New Jersey, which is considered an agricultural and industrial area. We grew up in the Lehigh Valley and the Delaware Water Gap, which are part of Pennsylvania and New Jersey.

Some of our fondest childhood memories are visiting the homes of both sets of grandparents, which were located on Montana Mountain and the Delaware River. Our maternal grandparents, who we affectionately called Nanny and Poppy Beagle, had a home on the mountain. Poppy built the house himself. We could roam free, play outdoors, and just breathe. We remember how beautiful the changing seasons were. In the fall, the mountain looked like it was on fire with vibrant orange, red, and yellow leaves. It was a majestic and unspoiled area.

One of our aunts married a dairy farmer, and they lived right around the corner from our grandparents. As kids, we learned to milk cows and play in the silos and haystacks. We thought our aunts hung the moon and were close to all three of them. They would often babysit us, even though they were not much older than we were.

Poppy was a World War II veteran. He was wounded in the war and returned home 100 percent disabled, struggling the remainder of his adult life with residual physical ailments and emotional problems. He suffered from post-traumatic stress disorder (PTSD), except in 1944 this disorder hadn't yet been discovered.

During the war, he had been shot in the shoulder and rear end. When he turned around, shrapnel exploded in his face. He'd been blinded immediately and soon fell unconscious, although he could hear the soldiers saying, "Beagle is dead." He woke up in the field hospital morgue, freezing cold and screaming for someone to find him.

When he was stabilized, he was sent home from Germany and admitted into Valley Forge Veterans Hospital in Pennsylvania. There, he endured numerous reconstructive surgeries to his face, including a steel plate inserted into his forehead, a false eye, and a reconstructed nose that left his face deformed.

Miraculously, he lived. As a child, our mom would regularly visit him in the hospital with Nanny. Before long, the VA became a second home to them. Poppy had multiple emotional breakdowns and was eventually hospitalized in the "asylum" for a number of years.

Sometimes his forehead swelled up to the size of a football, which then necessitated another surgery. One time, while a doctor was performing surgery, he found a piece of gauze that had accidentally been left from one of his surgeries in Germany. Periodically, he would have to get the fluid drained from his forehead.

He was awarded a Purple Heart for his bravery, courage, and service to our country. This medal is the highest of honors for anyone serving in the military, but it came at an indescribable sacrifice to my grandfather and his family.

After he returned home, sometimes he would hear a plane overhead and tackle Mom and Nanny to get them to safety. He insisted they quickly find shelter and crouch behind the sofa or under the kitchen table. Nanny would calm him down and explain that they were all safe and that it was just an airplane in the sky—no danger here.

Eventually, he began the climb back to health and sanity. He started working for a cement company as a truck driver, until one day an accident occurred. While unloading the truck, steel pipes fell onto him and broke his back. Poppy was in a full-body cast for six months.

As little girls, we remember Nanny showing us the newspaper article about Peter J. Beagle and the accident. He seemed indestructible indeed, always bouncing back from exceptionally difficult blows, both physically and mentally.

As for Nanny, she was timid and anxious, often observing life from the sidelines. I remember, however, that she had a great laugh. She also loved to play bingo. When we visited, we would go with her to bingo games located in a church basement, and the fun would begin. She would buy multiple bingo cards for the night and have all her daubers ready. It was exciting. We could feel the anticipation in the room as the bingo cards filled up.

When Nanny won at bingo, we were given strict instructions to fib about her winnings.

Poppy would ask, "How'd you do tonight?"

She would always answer, "I broke even," or "It was a slow night."

This was an affectionate game between the two of them. She enjoyed stashing her winnings in a coffee can for her next adventure to the bingo hall, and he happily encouraged this indulgence. It was sweet to watch their interactions.

***

Our mom was born in 1942. She had three sisters born in 1949, 1952, and 1954. Due to Poppy's World War II service, there is a seven-year age gap between our mom and her next sibling. Mom's younger sisters always wanted to be around her. They nicknamed her "Rosie," and she became a surrogate mother to them.

The school kids teased Mom, calling Poppy "monkey face." I can assure you no one did it twice because our mom had a fierce love and loyalty to her father. Anyone who had the gall to offend his honor got a whooping—from mom.

She was the apple of her dad's eye. They were extremely close, and we could always count on our grandparents for help. They were a stable support throughout all of the chaos and abuse we experienced in our family.

Despite his previous trauma and injuries, Poppy provided unconditional love to all of us, and he embodied a quiet strength, a gentle soul,
and a big heart. He would do anything to support our mom.

Our grandparents on our dad's side—Nanny and Poppy Burd—
owned and operated a fast-food stand that sold hot dogs, hamburgers,
and soft-serve ice cream. It was fun to visit there and get all the free food
we wanted!

They resided in Belvidere, New Jersey, and lived in a bungalow that
overlooked the Delaware River. It was cool because you had to descend a
steep ladder to get to the dock and beach. They bought us a motorboat,
and we learned to water ski in the summer months.

The home was located across the street from a graveyard and corn-
field. We played hide-and-seek in the cemetery as kids. Our cousins are
close to our age, and we loved spending time with them while in New
Jersey. We would set up a tent in the backyard and camp out, telling
ghost stories and freaking each other out! We had an endless supply of
delicious, fresh sweet corn, which we included in the menu for our outdoor picnics, celebrations, and parties.

Nanny Burd seemed strict and stern and carried herself with an air
of elegance. Her hair was always done in ways I considered, as a child,
to be fancy and stylish, which made her look very distinguished. Even
though she was petite, she had a tough exterior and could come across
as aloof.

Poppy Burd, on the other hand, was charismatic, gregarious, and
fun to be around. They liked to entertain, and we remember parties
down on the Delaware River.

Our dad described his parents as strict, and shared he was beaten
by his father as a child. Dad had a reputation as a "hellion" in adolescence. I know this was true and that my dad suffered childhood abuse.
Fortunately, my sisters and I experienced his parents as loving and kind,

and they opened their home to us without unleashing any physical anger.

By the time we were in our early teens, Poppy and Nanny Burd had moved to Florida because they needed a warmer climate due to health concerns. They managed a condo property on the Intracoastal Waterway in Pompano Beach.

It was a beautiful property, and we made friends with other families who were visiting. We played with the same kids each summer. It was fun to be exposed to other families from different cultures around the globe.

As we got older and into our teens, we had many shenanigans on the Ft. Lauderdale strip. The beach lifestyle and atmosphere were appealing to us and very different from the mountains.

We loved, loved, loved all four of our grandparents! Their homes were the two places we always felt safe and supported, no matter what.

Thank God for grandparents!

Family Secrets

There is a saying in recovery: "You are only as sick as your secrets." Well, based on that adage, our family was certifiable.

As children, we learned to keep secrets. Our parents never told us not to share the truth about our family with other adults, but it was unspoken. Besides, how do you go to a teacher, neighbor, relative, or friend and talk about the kind of violence that occurred in our home? The kind of violence that we regularly witnessed?

We lied for each other under the guise of protecting one another. We also lied because some secrets felt unspeakable. In addition to the secrets we witnessed firsthand, other family secrets circulated over the years. For example, we heard whispers that our great-grandfather had committed suicide when Poppy Burd was twelve years old.

The story was told that he went into the woods with a shotgun and did not return. Karen found out years later in adulthood from our grandmother that he ate rat poisoning and had a slow, painful, self-inflicted death. Apparently, making up a lie that he had shot himself was a better story than the truth.

Another family secret was regarding a suicide attempt by our father when he was twenty-three. By then, he had three children, ages five, four, three, and a fourth child on the way. He slit his wrists in the bathroom and was taken to a psychiatric facility and admitted for three days.

Karen, who was five at the time, has a memory of our mom taking us to visit and waving to Dad through a hospital window. We can't imagine the despair and confusion this caused for all parties involved. There was never another suicide attempt that we know of, and family members never discussed it.

Another secret no one discussed took place when Dad visited Karen in Florida. Karen and I were young adults at the time and living on our own. Our younger cousins were visiting at the same time. While inebriated, Dad made a pass at our cousin's fifteen-year-old friend. Everyone was appalled, upset, and disgusted. Karen had to deal with the fallout of his behavior with relatives. He said he blacked out and had no memory of the event. Everyone involved was afraid to confront him directly, and the incident was swept under the rug.

We sisters are fourth-generation alcoholics. As children, we did not recognize this.

We believed our Poppy Beagle drank daily to minimize and anesthetize his physical pain from his war injuries.

We knew Poppy Burd drank daily because he entertained frequently; therefore alcohol was part of his daily routine.

We were told that Dad drank daily because it was part of his "corporate culture" and work responsibilities.

Alcohol was in our home and consumed every day by the role models and adults in our lives.

We were raised to believe that drinking every day was normal and how all families operated.

Alcohol was our family tradition.

We didn't know any better.

3

The Seeds of Dysfunction

KELLY SPEAKS

Mom described my personality as a child as sensitive, rambunctious, and inquisitive. She described Karen as self-conscious, quiet, a loner, and loving. When I entered kindergarten, I was enrolled in speech therapy. I stuttered badly, and even my mom could not understand me. She had to ask Karen and Kendra what I was saying. My sisters always knew what I was trying to say, and they interpreted for our mom. Sometimes I wonder if this was the beginning of a lifelong pattern of feeling unseen and unheard, as if I had no voice.

My sisters and I went to the mat for each other often. We could tease each other, but no one else had better try. As a child, Kendra was awkward, overweight, and wore thick glasses. Mean kids would call her "four eyes" and "fatty." Our last name was Burd, and I remember other creative insults like "Burd Brain" and "Burd Turd." It hurt me to see kids be so mean to one another, especially my sister. I wanted to protect and defend her.

I also wanted to take care of my mom. When I was in first grade, we had a class assignment to write a letter to Santa Claus, which was very exciting! The letter I wrote was brief and got published in the local newspaper. I remember I wrote something like this:

Dear Santa:
Please bring my mommy some nice, new clothes.
She always takes care of us. If it's okay, I'd like a Mr. Potato Head.

Mom put her kids' needs first, and we didn't want for anything. She was a talented seamstress and made a lot of our clothing. I loved holidays because she would dress us all up in new clothes and outfits. I remember my favorite Easter outfit. All four of us dressed up in capes, gloves, and hats that she made. So fun! Mom seemed to have an endless supply of love for us. She always told me I was special and smart and could succeed at anything I put my mind to.

Dad, on the other hand, was strict and critical of all of us. It seemed we just never did anything up to his standards.

I remember one day he told us to go outside and rake the leaves in the front yard. We were all between the ages of seven and nine. Immediately, we began having fun raking the leaves in piles and jumping in them. Dad came out of the house and started yelling at us. He told us we were not raking properly. He grabbed one of the rakes and told us to rake the lawn "this" way. I didn't understand his reasoning because the outcome was the same. Who cared how we got the leaves picked up?

As we watched his anger grow, it halted when he stepped on the fanned side of the rake. With that one step, the handle flew up and hit him on the forehead. After he finished yelling at us and went inside the house, my sisters and I busted a gut laughing.

We often made fun of him behind his back. Sometimes he would wag his finger at us and begin to walk out of the room, then turn around and say, "And another thing . . ." We would mock and imitate him as soon as he left the room.

All of us girls were stubborn. We found ways to survive. The mocking of our dad was our way of tipping the scale for the things we couldn't make fun of—the things that hurt too much.

For example, Dad would say things like, "Why don't you girls go out and play in traffic?" While this was said in jest and was supposed to be funny, it wasn't. He also referred to us as "mistakes," which made us feel very unwanted. I always felt like a burden to my father and knew that he would rather have been footloose and fancy-free.

When I was in my senior year of high school, Dad asked me what I might want to do for a career. I said I wasn't sure but knew that I wanted to help people. Maybe I would work at a home for the elderly.

"Go ahead and try that," he snarled. "Get that shit out of your system because you will never make any money at it."

I was devastated. He couldn't see me for who I was or encourage my interests.

While often cruel to my sisters and me, Dad was handsome, charismatic, and a great salesman. Coworkers admired him and enjoyed being around him. He was successful in his career and was eventually promoted to vice president of sales for a nationally known chemical company. Every time he got promoted—every three to five years—we relocated to a new region of the country.

My parents tried to put a positive spin on each relocation, telling us that moving so often would give us skills as adults to relate to any person or situation. But the frequent moves were devastating to my sisters and me. We felt like we never fit in. It was a losing battle to put down roots, and we were forced to adapt to new schools, friends, and environments continuously.

I remember visiting our grandparents in Florida during a summer vacation. While we were there, my parents announced we would be moving yet again. I comforted all three of my sisters as they cried. I hugged them, told them we had each other, and we would be okay.

When I got them calmed down, I locked myself into the bathroom and cried like a baby on the floor. The tile was cold, hard, and unforgiving as I knelt and put my hands over my face to cover up my sobbing. I would not allow anyone to see me showing weakness or emotion. Displaying strength was my role in the family. I took care of everybody else and was acutely aware of my surroundings and the needs of others. I had to be strong because it seemed that everything around us was uncertain.

One time when I was very young, we were at my grandparents' house on the river, and they were having a party. My dad, who had been drinking heavily, kissed another woman in front of everyone. As you can imagine, this was very confusing to me. I noticed that Mom was nowhere to be found. I went looking for her and found her across the street in the graveyard. She was sitting on the ground by a headstone, crying. I remember comforting her, and we walked hand in hand back to the party.

To see my mother so upset was extremely traumatic for me. Even though I was too young to understand fully what was happening, to have my dad publicly disrespect and embarrass my mother felt unbearable. It rocked my sense of safety and security.

As we got older and began to test our independence, Dad became more violent and demeaning. By then, we knew he habitually cheated on Mom. He earned a reputation as a womanizer and never tried to hide it. When we went out to dinner as a family, he would flirt with the waitresses, who were often close to our ages. My sisters and I always knew which secretary he was cheating with because they would be overly attentive to us at company picnics.

Throughout my childhood, I witnessed women taking on subservient roles, being objectified, and treated like sex objects by my father. I thought it was disgusting behavior and felt humiliated for Mom, who seemed to ignore it or take it in stride.

Dad once said that he beat us to make us strong. I don't advise this! We were always on edge, waiting until the next blowout. My home life was extremely chaotic and unpredictable.

I was told to stuff my feelings. As a result, I never trusted my judgment and felt angry and resentful all the time. My sisters and I never had friends over. I was acutely depressed as a teenager because of the anger I kept inside and the frustrations I had toward my dad. Not to mention, it was overwhelming carrying the emotional load for my sisters, who relied on me for support.

The level of shame that his constant disapproval and belittling caused us would take years to resolve.

KAREN SPEAKS

The first time we moved was from Bethlehem, Pennsylvania, to Alexandria, Virginia. Our ages at the time were twelve, eleven, ten, and seven.

We loved living in Bethlehem because we fit right in with the families of steelworkers and farmers. Our grandparents, aunts, uncles, and cousins lived in the area too. We were treated like we were special. There were fun Christmas celebrations and wonderful family gatherings.

During the move, I cried for two straight weeks and was inconsolable. We moved into the biggest house we had ever lived in, complete with four bedrooms, three bathrooms and a built-in swimming pool in the backyard. But the big house didn't matter. We just wanted to go back home to our previous life in Pennsylvania. We had left behind the comfort of the mountain and the support of our grandparents, who would become our base camp for many years to come.

I remember my first day of seventh grade at my new school. I wore a pink pantsuit with little white and gray flowers on it. I loved that pantsuit and thought it was beautiful. When I got to school, I felt like I had been throat punched. All the boys and girls were wearing jeans and T-shirts. I felt like such a country bumpkin. It was the first time I remember feeling like a nobody.

I cried when I got home and begged Mom to take me shopping for new clothes, which she did.

I don't think Mom wanted to move away from our old home either.

Somehow, I made it through seventh and eighth grade. By ninth grade, I had a few friends but was never one of the popular kids. I did not play sports or fit in with any of the high school cliques. My sisters were my best friends.

I decided I wanted to be a cheerleader because they were pretty and popular. I went to every practice and spent hours memorizing cheers and jumps. I was so nervous on tryout day and was devastated when I didn't make the team. Mom tried to comfort me by telling me all the other girls had an advantage because their moms were on the PTA and involved in school politics, but I knew I was simply not good enough.

I am embarrassed now to admit how much that affected me. I began intentionally missing the bus so I could stay home from school. Avoiding school solved one problem but created another. Whenever Dad was home, he drank, and the tension was thick at our house. We walked on eggshells all the time.

I started sneaking out.

I remember my first drinking experience like it happened yesterday. I snuck out one night and went to a party in the woods with a few of the popular kids. There were three girls, three boys, grain alcohol, Southern Comfort, and Crush Cherry Soda. I drank that stuff like it was Kool-Aid.

I remember the warm glow of alcohol going down my throat and into my stomach. For the first time since our move, I felt popular and cute and part of the in-crowd. Alcohol made me feel comfortable and at ease. With this buzz, I fit in and all was right in the world.

I loved that feeling.

I had found that sweet spot of the alcohol experience and would chase it for years and years to come.

That night I also experienced my first blackout. I was grateful that someone brought me home and didn't leave me behind in the woods. I was extremely sick the next day and did not remember anything. My mother told me I had thrown up outside the house, inside the house, and all over myself and that she had cleaned me up. I had dry heaves for three days afterward. I now know that this was alcohol poisoning.

That was the first time I swore I would never drink like that again, the first time I swore off alcohol . . . until the next opportunity to drink came along. I was hooked on feeling that sweet spot.

How I wanted to be there again!

KELLY SPEAKS

Our move to Virginia was the first move of many as my father worked his way up the corporate ladder. Image was important to him. It seemed to me that as he started earning more money, our family started to unravel.

Also, neither one of our parents were prepared for our preteen and teenage years. As we began to mature and assert our independence, our father's dictatorial style no longer worked. His rage and abuse escalated.

Karen was a straight A student through eighth grade. I remember her working hard to gain Dad's approval. He liked basketball, so she would memorize his favorite players' stats, hoping to impress him when they watched games together.

Young and naïve, she kept trying to figure out how to make new friends and fit in with her peers. After several attempts to fit in with the jocks and cheerleaders, she gravitated toward the misfits, the low hanging fruit—kids, like us, who didn't fit in. Things went south quickly.

One night Karen had some girlfriends sleeping over. This was a rare occasion because we typically didn't have friends visit the house. An exception was made to celebrate Karen's birthday. My dad found a six-pack of beer under her bed. Furious, he called each parent and insisted they pick up their kids and take them home. Karen's friends felt sorry for her because they saw Dad yelling and screaming and knew she was in a world of trouble. After they left, he beat her senseless.

I witnessed a lot of violence toward my mother and Karen. At eight years old, I started calling the police on my father. Sometimes I tried to intervene when he was beating my mother. These events would haunt me for years to come. I carried guilt for not being able to stop the beatings. When I became an adult, I learned through therapy and professional training that these events I experienced created trauma.

Below are two poems I wrote in an attempt to make sense of the repeated violence I witnessed as a child.

Witness

I am a witness.
Witness to the shame and humiliation caused by my mother's black eyes and welts on her face as we walk into the grocery store.
I see the stares, but no one seems to care.
No one ever asks what happened.

I am a witness to my sister's beating that left dark bruises
and marks all over her neck and chest.
I watch as she struggles to pick out the right shirt for school the next morning. One that won't show the bruising. She cannot cover her neck but uses makeup to lessen the color of her bruises. She goes to school. She doesn't want to have to explain. She knows she will lie. She is angry. No one ever asks what happened.

Beaten

I am asleep.
I awaken to a loud *thud*
While hearing, *I'm going to knock your lights out!*
I'm scared. Who has fallen to the floor?

I jump out of bed, run upstairs, and see my mom laying on the floor unconscious. I'm scared. My father stands over her, crying, yelling, *Rose, get up, get up.* She opens her eyes and cries, is beaten and helpless with her four children standing close by.

My father gets ice and begins to tend to her black eye and the swelling on her face. Wipes the blood from her broken lip.

My sisters and I are young, helpless. We are all crying now. Things calm down. My mom is okay and asks us to go back to bed. My father tucks us in, crying, full of sadness and promises never to hurt my mom again.

He kisses us good night.

We were silenced by fear and shame of the secrets we kept as a family—bound by the code of silence. We stopped having friends over. We stopped being invited to friends' sleepovers. We never knew when or why the next outburst would happen. We tried our best to behave.

We had each other, and that was enough.

Karen's rebellion began to increase. She would confront our dad for his drinking and faults. She ran away from home on several occasions.

Mom ran interference and, I believe, purposefully took beatings for her.

All of my parents' attention and energy seemed to go toward Karen.

One afternoon, Dad told me to get in the car because we needed to go look for Karen. When we found her hanging out at the 7-Eleven, she was smoking a cigarette and talking to some boys. To me, this seemed like normal adolescent behavior.

Dad got out of the car, pulled her hair, and began dragging her to the car. When he got her into the car, he said, "If you are going to act like a dog in heat, I'll treat you like one."

After violent episodes, Mom would put us all in the car with our dog, Duchess, a German Shepherd, and an antique rocking chair, then proceed to drive us home to New Jersey. Why we needed the rocking chair, no one knows.

We were always relieved to be back on the mountain, our haven. We would stay a week or so and then go home to Dad, and we girls never understood why.

This was our childhood, and things would soon go from bad to worse.

4

The Nut House

KAREN SPEAKS

At the end of my freshman year, my parents told us that we were moving again. We cried and pouted, but it made no difference. Another promotion for Dad. Another new school for us.

Living in Virginia, we had been just four hours from our family in Pennsylvania. But now we were moving to the suburbs of Chicago, Illinois, much farther away. I felt like we would never see our family again.

I just wanted to go home to Pennsylvania. A place where I knew the rules.

We moved that summer. Boy, was I angry.

I started smoking weed and drinking whenever possible, and it seemed to be possible a lot. I would skip school often. We could miss ten days of a class before being tossed out. I remember showing up to my gym class on the tenth day, and when the teacher kicked me out, I said, "But I only missed nine days." I was always trying to outsmart the powers that be. And often I did.

I was beginning to hone my manipulation skills.

A few months into my sophomore year, I had already run away a couple of times, gotten in some trouble with the police, and started cutting myself. My parents thought I should see a psychiatrist. In the seventies, "messing with someone's brain" was a new science and new idea.

The term *crazy* had been thrown at me, and that just made me angrier. I was pretty sure my parents were the crazy ones. Couldn't anyone else see what went on in our house? I knew my sisters did, but they were afraid of punishment, and I didn't blame them. So, I acted out enough for all of us. And I got punished—a lot.

The ultimate punishment for me was being sent to a psychiatric hospital. It shall affectionately be called the Nut House from here on. I was admitted against my will. Of course, will doesn't matter when you are a teenager because everyone has power over you. I was stripped of my own choices. I was defenseless.

This place was *not* a rehab facility (rehabs weren't trendy until the 1980s). No, this was a full-blown Nut House. My dad's insurance company paid every cent of the bill, so there was no rush to get me home.

The insurance company required a diagnosis to continue paying the bill, and my diagnoses ranged from manic-depressive disorder, borderline personality disorder, neurotic, and many other things that were not an accurate diagnosis. I never believed any of it, but I learned to use the labels to justify my belligerent attitude and behavior. In fact, those labels became such an ingrained part of my identity that they haunted me my whole life and shadowed me well into my thirties.

My first stint was six months. Surprisingly, I made friends, went to school, and became amazingly comfortable there. I loved my shrink because he was kind—I had a daddy complex, after all. I looked forward to seeing him on session days, which occurred once or twice a week for ten minutes. Every session ended with him prescribing more medication.

Every day, nurses would dispense the pills, checking under my tongue to make sure I swallowed. I was given enough medication to knock out a horse.

I finally started to see the game and did not want to play it anymore. I vowed that somehow, some way I would reclaim my power.

I was, by most standards, still an innocent kid. The other kids in the hospital had been in more trouble than me. I met a twelve-year-old arsonist, schizophrenic teenagers, and generally messed-up people. I fantasized that one day I would be the queen of an island, and all the misunderstood children could live there and be healed by love. Then, everyone would want us because we would all be fixed.

It is remarkable that forty-five years later, I remember the other children I met there. The bond we shared will last forever, even if we never see each other again. It is sad because I know that our bond was created because of our pain.

I learned a lot from the other girls at the Nut House. I learned about all kinds of drugs I had never tried. I learned more about boys and sex. When we broke the rules, we had to deal with staff we called the Goon Squad. They were the guys who fought you and held you down so the nurse could give you a Thorazine shot and knock you out.

One day, a few of us decided we were going to escape. Looking back, it was like an episode of *The Three Stooges*. We were in a locked ward that was five floors up. The elevators had keys. The only way out was through the emergency door exits at the end of each hallway. I don't think we believed we would make it out when we started this adventure but—to our amazement—we did.

One of us pushed the emergency door, and we ran as fast as we could down five flights of stairs out onto the Chicago Street of Lake Shore Drive, the Goon Squad close behind.

We came out into the parking lot, and I remember making myself ridiculously small and hiding behind the tire of a car so no one would see my feet. After a while, the Goon Squad gave up and went inside.

I do not know how many of us got caught, but I did not. Some of us found each other and began walking out of the city. One of the girls, who really did need medication and treatment, managed to make it out with us. She just followed behind. Poor thing had that thousand-yard, glassy-eyed stare. But she was one of us, so we took special care of her.

We hadn't thought very far ahead, and had no plan of where to go if we escaped. We had no money for trains or busses, so we started hitchhiking.

Eventually, the police saw us and picked us up. They kept asking who we were and where we were from, but we would not give up the information. When we were finally scared enough to tell them, they did not believe our story and laughed. So much for telling the truth. Who in their right mind would believe that five teenage girls escaped from a nut house and got away with it?

They called the hospital and confirmed our story. Then they called our parents.

I cried so hard when Mom picked me up from the police station that she let me stay home overnight and didn't take me back to the Nut House until the next day. My punishment was three days in five-point restraints with food and bathroom breaks. Crazy stuff.

The other punishment we all dreaded was the mysterious quiet room. It was a tiny room with a mattress on the floor. No kidding, on the floor. It had a small window allowing the nurses to observe the patient. The quiet room is where you went after a Thorazine shot for twenty-four hours to calm down.

Shortly after the great escape, the professionals recommended to my parents that I receive electroconvulsive therapy (ECT). This was commonly known as electric shock therapy and was quite popular in the 1970s. I am eternally grateful that my parents did not authorize that treatment for me.

I did, however, watch through the window of our room one day as my roommate was strapped down for an ECT treatment. I was petrified. Staff put a bite guard in her mouth and electrodes on her head. Her body violently convulsed. That image stayed in my head for a very long time. I could not imagine what that "therapy" did to her brain.

My mother and sisters came to see me religiously. I could always count on them. My mom would bring me snacks to keep in my room and share with the other patients.

I didn't realize at the time how blessed I was. Many of the kids had been abandoned and rejected, and no one came to visit them.

I had no clue why I did the things I did. I think I wanted to make my parents feel as bad as I did and wanted the world to hurt as much as it seemed to hurt me. I tried to manipulate every situation. Sometimes when I called home, I threatened my mother, saying, "If you don't get me out of here, I will kill myself!" I guess I thought that threatening suicide would gain me some special attention and a measure of control over my life. It didn't work. After these threats, my hysterical mom called back and spoke to the nurses, which meant more Thorazine, quiet rooms, and restraints for me.

I piled a lot of guilt on my mother, which I wholeheartedly regret today. My parents loved me and did the best that they knew how at the time. I have no excuses except to say that I did not know any different. If you don't *know* different, you can't do different.

At long last, after six months I went home. My parents divorced around this time, but I do not remember if it was before or after my homecoming. I do remember the relief I felt when Dad moved out. The butterflies in my stomach were gone. We could relax at home and not be afraid.

I came out of the Nut House with a whole new skill set, having learned from girls who were far more sophisticated and streetwise than me. After I was released, I started trying every drug under the sun. The local high school did not want me back, so I was homeschooled for a few hours a day. Fine by me. It gave me more time to do what I wanted to do.

Still heavily medicated, I continued outpatient visits with my psychiatrist, who I had always looked forward to seeing while institutionalized. After a few months, however, he referred me to another local teen shrink. He told my mother he could not continue seeing me because I was a delightful child and he was no longer objective about my treatment. Strange, right? Years later, I read in the newspaper that he had been arrested for molesting some of his young female patients. Thankfully, I was not one of them. I do not know what happened to him, but I pray with all my heart that he paid dearly for hurting girls who were so vulnerable and raw and who trusted him.

I spent the next year and a half in and out of psychiatric facilities. It was all more of the same. Most staff were kind and understanding. Their jobs were not high paying, so most of them were in their young twenties. Vulnerable teenage girls and male staffers in their twenties. What could go wrong?

I developed a crush on a staff member who worked closely with me. He would give me presents occasionally and made me feel special. After I was discharged, I continued a relationship with him. There were no boundaries—we used drugs together and were attracted to one another. He kissed me and I panicked because I was still a virgin. I was scared because he was eight years older than me and so much more experienced. Things fizzled out quickly.

During one of my hospitalizations, there was an internal investigation involving a young male staffer who worked the overnight shift. My roommate had accused him of molestation.

A female staff member gently confronted me and asked if I had experienced any type of unusual behavior from this man. I admitted that I had. He fondled me during late-night bed checks. I never would have said anything to anyone because I felt too unworthy. I did not understand how wrong that was. As a result of the investigation, he was fired.

There was little valuable therapy at these places. I became institutionalized and got comfortable. I thought this must be what a boarding school dorm felt like. I felt more at home there than I did at my actual home.

The lives of my sisters and my mother went on without me. When I came home for good, I did not know if they were glad or not. I knew my family loved me, and I loved them deeply, but when I finally came home, it was a huge adjustment for all of us.

KELLY SPEAKS

Another move. This time to Barrington, Illinois. We moved into a huge house, and each of us got our own bedroom. The high school had over two thousand students. It was an affluent area, and we were surrounded by rich kids.

Another place where we did not fit in.

I was jealous of Karen. I would study, outline, memorize, and make a B; she never studied and made straight As. Still, somehow I knew that, despite my struggles to learn, education was my way to a better life. On top of this, Karen got all the attention from boys. They didn't even notice me when she was around.

Karen could act out—and boy, did she.

School seemed an annoying distraction from Karen's real interests, which were drugs, alcohol, and rebellion in any form. She was out of control. One day she pulled a knife on my father and threatened to kill him. She often overdosed on drugs from my parents' medicine cabinet. She self-harmed, cut, and burned her arms. During one of her many stints in a hospital unit, she broke a light bulb and slit her wrists in a locked, secure psychiatric facility.

Karen's wild behaviors meant she was the focus of *everything*. All my mother's actions—all of her time and energy—revolved around Karen. We scheduled our lives around family therapy sessions. And when Karen was hospitalized in downtown Chicago, my youngest sister and I made the hour drive with Mom every night from Barrington to downtown Chicago.

I watched as my sister's illness and treatment took a toll on our mother's health and well-being. My mother had a neurological disorder that worsened under duress. Her head and hands would shake involuntarily. This was a barometer for measuring when my mom was close to her breaking point.

My mother would have given her own life to save Karen's in order to make her well. How I wanted to wave a magic wand and heal my mother's sense of failure, confusion, and inability to help a daughter she loved dearly.

Unfortunately, I didn't see any successful outcomes for my sister. None of the interventions through therapy or medicine helped her. Instead, I watched as my beautiful older sister, my best friend, went into these hospitals a naive, innocent virgin and came out a promiscuous, manipulative drug addict.

Her behavior was outrageous, and her self-loathing was endless. Consequently, she carried the stigma attached to words like *crazy, disturbed, mentally ill,* and *druggie* for most of her life. I felt sorry for her. I loved her. I wanted to do anything possible to minimize the pain she was feeling.

I was stuck in the middle between my mom and sister. I lied and covered up for Karen for years. I would excuse her behavior, no matter how outrageous. One year, Karen came home for a holiday visit at Christmas. My mom had bought Karen a fashionable pair of boots, but when she tried them on the zipper wouldn't close on her upper calf. She had gained about fifty pounds given all the psychotropic medications she was on. She threw the boots across the room and started crying and yelling. Merry Christmas to us.

After another home visit, Mom and I dropped Karen off at the hospital. In the lobby, before going through the body-check process, Karen told the nurse she had to go to the bathroom. The nurse directed me to go to the bathroom with Karen to supervise her. When we got to the toilet, Karen took a bag of marijuana from her pocket and shoved it up her vagina. She said to me if I told anyone, she would beat my ass. I didn't tell anyone. I carried guilt about this for years. I'm sure she was quite popular on the unit that evening.

Dad visited Karen in the hospital a few times. His visits ended with him refusing to engage in any therapy. This just added to Karen's sense of worthlessness. He couldn't participate constructively and wasn't willing to evaluate his part in our family dysfunction. He left and moved out to live with his secretary. I remember wanting to throw a party when my dad moved out.

We could finally breathe knowing everyone was safe.

5

They Say You Can't Go Home Again

KELLY SPEAKS

Hallelujah! Hallelujah! Hall-le-lu-jah!

After seventeen years, my parents were getting divorced. Seventeen years of us watching our father cheat, beat, and abuse our mother.

My sisters and I were thrilled. My youngest sister struggled the most over the divorce, perhaps because we had tried to shield her as much as possible from the violence. But those of us who had lived the brunt of it? We were ecstatic.

We moved from a five-bedroom home into a small townhouse where we shared bedrooms. My mother, with no formal education or work experience, began looking for a job.

After completing an associate degree, she found work as a secretary. I was so proud of my mom! She excelled in her work environment, though she constantly worried about paying the bills.

Mom was overwhelmed anytime Dad was nearby. He overpowered her emotionally and physically, and she was unable to defend herself.

One time after Dad had moved out, he came over to the townhouse and started berating Mom. I came down into the kitchen and told him that he didn't live here anymore and didn't have the right to treat Mom this way. I told him he could leave or stay and be civil. He left. I was scared to confront him but felt it was my responsibility.

Mom had sole responsibility for disciplining us. We did not fear her, and we were unruly. Mom had poor boundaries and was under a tremendous amount of pressure. Her head bobbed, and her hands shook continuously.

Mom didn't know how to say no. To us, *no* meant keep badgering her until we wore her down and she gave in. This meant we could do *what* we wanted *when* we wanted—with no accountability.

This was dangerous with a house full of teenagers, one of whom had learned far too much about how far she could push the limits.

I was put in a position to tell on Kendra and Karen frequently. I wanted to decrease my mom's stress, but then my sisters labeled me a narc. This put me in an impossible position.

One day, Mom found a bong hidden underneath the bathroom sink and asked me what it was. I told her it was used to smoke pot and get high. She told me to take it outside and throw it in the dumpster. She asked me where Kendra and Karen's drug stash was, and I took her down to the basement. I lifted the ceiling tiles and took out my sisters' weed. This wasn't the only hiding place, but I only needed one to appease her. I knew I would be in trouble with Karen and Kendra, but what choice did I have?

I shared a room with our youngest sister, Kolleen. At night we played a game.

"Who loves you?" I would ask her before answering my own question, saying, "I do, forever and ever and ever."

We tried to shelter Kolleen from the violence and abuse we suffered. She was young and vulnerable, and we did our best to take care of her. She wanted to hang out with my friends and boyfriend in high school, and I let her. She looked up to me, and I loved her dearly.

I had taken on the role of the "parentified child" by this time. This role is typically taken by the oldest child in an alcoholic family. Given our family circumstances and Karen being sick, I moved into the role as caretaker for my mother and sisters.

In the meantime, high school was hell for me, and I hated it. Karen was in and out of psychiatric hospitals. Both older sisters were stoners. They skipped school and earned terrible reputations.

At the beginning of my freshman year, the principal called me into his office.

"Kelly, the faculty will be watching you," he warned. "We won't tolerate the type of disruption your two older sisters have caused for the school."

I knew he was trying to scare me straight, but his words made me angry.

"It's not fair for you to stereotype me based on my sisters," I shot back. "I'm not like them. I think drinking and doing drugs is stupid."

Indeed, I had no desire to be like my sisters. I stayed away from it all. I didn't fit in with the jocks or the freaks. I had one or two best friends, and that was enough for me. I kept my head down, made good grades, and graduated in three years.

I confess I felt a sweet satisfaction when the principal had to approve my early graduation.

I was in my freshman year when I met my first love, a boy who was a senior. He had enlisted in the military and left for basic training immediately after graduation. Despite being separated, we dated for two more years. During that time, I hung out frequently with my boyfriend's best friend, who became like a brother to my sisters and me.

But more often than not I stayed home nights and weekends, waiting for the phone to ring, hoping it would be my boyfriend. Because he was away in the Army, I never went to a high school dance, attended prom, or socialized in high school. I hung out with my mom, learned to crochet, and spent time reading, isolating myself.

My boyfriend was stationed at Fort Knox, Kentucky, where his family had originated. When his family decided to move back to Kentucky, they invited me to move with them.

It was a significant decision, a crossroad, and I knew in my heart it was not the direction I wanted for my life. We broke up after three years of dating.

Looking back, I think I was a depressed teenager. I had chronic stomach aches, kidney infections, headaches, and other somatic complaints. Being ill seemed like an acceptable way to express my distress and get my mom's attention.

In addition, I was recognized for my school performance. I knew that going to college was my path to a better life. Kendra and I graduated High School in 1980, and our family would move back to Pennsylvania. I didn't want to go back but didn't think I had any choice.

KAREN SPEAKS

When it came to road trips, Mom was fearless. She was not afraid to put four kids, our dog, and furniture in an old car and drive 1200 miles. She made the decision to move us back to Pennsylvania to be closer to her family. So we packed up our house, rented a truck, and hit the road again. After seven years, we were finally going back to the people, mountains, and rural area we loved.

We were going home!

Leaving Illinois was bittersweet. We were all teenagers, so there were sweet boyfriends and crushes left behind. You know, the ones you imagined yourself growing old with, the ones who got away. We shared tearful goodbyes and promises to stay in touch, but sadly never did. To this day, hearing certain songs still evokes memories of my first crush.

That road trip is one of my most cherished memories. We played stupid games and ate all kinds of snacks, stopping at Stuckey's for milkshakes along the way. We sang lots of songs, and to this day we can harmonize to "Going to the Chapel."

We got silly and slap happy.

"If you girls don't stop fighting right now, I'll turn this car around!" Mom would threaten. But we knew she loved it too.

When we finally pulled into town, we were hit with old memories and awaited new experiences.

It was the summer of 1980 in Lehigh Valley, Pennsylvania. That summer, Billy Joel's song "Allentown" became the local anthem.

But the fantasy and reality of going home again was like night and day. For starters, we soon discovered that most of the friends we had known in elementary school had long moved away. And the town seemed depressed. Men were out of work due to steel mills and manufacturing jobs being cut. I was fresh from the Nut House and desperate for a clean start, but I wasn't the only one who needed a job.

I had only been home a few weeks when I got loaded and got in my car to drive to Nanny Beagle's house to spend the night. I missed the turn on a winding country road and crashed my car. Somehow, I managed to drive the car safely to her house. I was lucky like that. The go-to excuse in that area when you had an accident was to say you hit a deer. No matter the damage to the car, barring any lamed deer on the road, you stuck to the story.

Without a working car, I had to find a job close enough for me to walk to. I landed one in the trimming department of Clyde's shirt factory.

We started at some crazy hour like 6:30 a.m. On my first day of work, I found out I had to buy my own pair of trimming scissors from them. I could not believe I had to pay for them out of my first paycheck. During my lunch break, I walked to the pizza place across the street, unable to decide if I wanted to finish the day or toss the whole job. After lunch, I went back to work because I needed money and, at that point, had no other plan.

Alcohol still played a huge role in our family. It was normal to drink at all functions, weekends, and especially on holidays. I grew up believing every family did that. Everyone got drunk, blacked out, and made fools of themselves, providing fodder for the family gossip mill until the next event.

One day I reached out to a girl who had been my best friend back when we were twelve. She invited me to hang out with her, her boyfriend, and some other friends. I was so excited at the prospect of having my old best friend back and making new friends!

The night started out fine, and, of course, we got our hands on some booze. I got so drunk that night, the next time I called her, she told me I was not the girl she used to know and was not interested in being my friend.

Ouch! That hurt! I buried it along with all my other pain and got angry. Anger was much easier for me to handle than letting myself feel vulnerable or hurt. That was for weak people, and I was far from weak, or so I thought. Big tough teenager, right? Nobody was going to tell me what to do anymore.

I never considered what I was putting my family through. I could only see the world as it spun around me. I was arrogant and extremely self-centered. Some of my attitude problems were from being a teenager, but most of it came from being an alcoholic in bloom. But who sees an alcoholic when they look at a teenage girl who is still cute and bubbly? Who believed alcoholism was a disease and not just a complete moral failing? Not me.

I started feeling more and more boxed in. Some of my extended family received government assistance, along with many people in the area. At the factory, I worked with people in their late teens who had kids and struggled for food and housing.

I knew I had to get out of there or I'd spend my life working the sewing machines. I'd end up drinking at the corner bar with my old man. I'd wear polyester stretch pants, have gray hair, and be a grandma when I was in my thirties.

We'd only been home for a few months, and I wanted out. I had no money, no car, and no place to go. School would be too much of an effort on my part, so I scratched that idea. What was there left to try?

One day I was walking home from work when a car pulled up beside me. I peered inside and broke into a big grin. It was Poppy and Nanny Burd, driving into town for a surprise visit from Florida.

My grandfather always had a soft spot for me. He would tell people I was his favorite, which made me feel bad because

I thought it hurt my sisters' feelings. After I told them my sob story, they invited me to come to Florida to visit them. I could drive back with them when they went home.

I said, "Hell, yes!"

I knew my family loved me, but I am sure they were relieved that I was leaving. No one tried to stop me. I left Pennsylvania with my grandparents, drove to sunny Florida, got sand in my shoes, and never looked back.

KELLY SPEAKS

After high school, my SAT scores weren't that good, so I attended community college in Northampton, Pennsylvania, for two years, earning straight As.

I was eligible to transfer my credits to complete my bachelor's degree in Pennsylvania or Virginia. I could claim residency in either state because my dad lived in Virginia. I chose Richmond. I wanted to get as far away as possible from Karen and the depressed area of Northampton.

Karen was still wreaking havoc in our family. Her drinking was out of control, and I shared a room with her. One night, she came home loaded and proceeded to pee in the bedroom closet. I was so angry. She had no memory of it in the morning. I remember telling my mother, "Either she goes or I go." My mother never needed to choose because my sister moved to Florida shortly after this incident, and I left for college.

Woo-hoo! College, here I come!

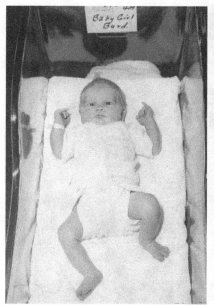 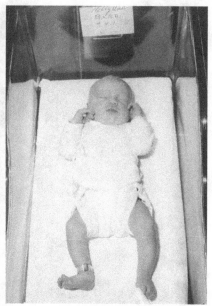

Karen, first born, July 22, 1961   *Kelly, third born, September 19, 1963*

Karen's first day of kindergarten   *Kelly's first day of kindergarten*

Karen's first Holy Communion

Kelly's first Holy Communion

Easter Sunday: Ages 3, 2, 1

*Hey Look, Kolleen's arrived! Karen, 11,
Kendra, 10, Kelly, 9, and Kolleen, 6*

*Mom was a talented
seamstress,
and we loved our Easter
outfits.*

Karen's high school photo

Kelly's high school photo

6

Adventures Beyond the Nest

KELLY SPEAKS

I enrolled at Virginia Commonwealth University. VCU had an excellent reputation for education majors, and I planned to get my degree in special education.

Upon arriving, I'd been assigned an off-campus apartment due to overcrowding in the dorms. Initially, I had been disappointed. Then I realized my off-campus apartment complex was party central! Every weekend there was free entertainment, where famous bands like The Allman Brothers performed, and it seemed like keggars were available twenty-four seven. Anytime, anywhere. The best part was this apartment had no adult supervision.

I loved being away from home. I loved having a newfound freedom. I loved meeting students from all over the United States.

I had zero experience drinking alcohol and never experimented in high school. One day, that all changed.

"Here." My new roomie handed me a beer as if it was the most natural thing in world.

I held the cold can in my hand and stared, not quite sure what to do next.

Students were partying all around me.

What the heck, I thought, then popped the tab. Eureka! I can't say I liked the taste, but I sure liked the feeling alcohol gave me. I was relaxed and at ease with myself and others.

From the beginning, I drank to get a buzz. Was there any other reason to drink? I could not relate to people who only had a drink or two and declared themselves social drinkers. What is that? Why would anyone drink like that?

Did I blackout in college? Certainly. Did I pee my pants when I was wasted? Sure. Did I puke my guts out? Definitely. Did I think it was all fun and games? Without a doubt. I thought getting wasted was just part of the normal college experience.

I met my second love in college. He was handsome, charismatic, and the life of the party. Sound familiar? We dated for four years, got engaged, and broke up. He was a creative graphic design artist. My boyfriend, best friend, and I came to be known as the three musketeers. We were inseparable. I learned over time that he was a self-centered womanizer. I thought I deserved better, and we broke things off. Another bullet dodged!

I got through college on student loans. I was invested in doing well and committed to academics. I studied hard and partied hard through college. I graduated Cum Laude. At the same time, it was not easy to navigate all the responsibilities that came with being independent. I was a cocktail waitress and worked at a local pancake house. There was always some type of drama going on with my friends.

By then, Mom had remarried, and she and my stepdad, Jerry—one of the best things to ever happen to our family—would visit often. Pennsylvania was a six-hour drive, and if I needed them, all I had to do was ask. Mom would bring freshly made apple pies for my roomies and me. Jerry (aka MacGyver) made me a beautiful wooden armoire to store all my clothes in and personally delivered it. He is a talented carpenter and handyman. They were both incredibly supportive of me. It felt good to know they were proud of me, and it was comforting to know I could count on them.

KAREN SPEAKS

My first few weeks in Florida were a slice of heaven. My grandparents managed a condo complex that was located on the Intracoastal Waterway. Location, location, location. To my delight, the boats and yachts would use the drawbridge at the Hillsboro Inlet. It is one of the most beautiful settings on earth.

Their complex was full of ritzy senior citizens, so my grandparents were very conscious of what these people thought of us. I respected my grandparents and did not want to hurt them, so I tried extremely hard to be a good girl. I hung around the pool and went to the beach. I missed my mom and sisters terribly. I would call my mother almost every night, but going back home was out of the question.

Fort Lauderdale Beach, affectionately referred to as Fort Liquordale by the locals, was the hot spot for spring break, and there were trendy bars on the strip. It just so happened that the legal drinking age was nineteen. Guess how old I was? That's right, nineteen.

I did not know anyone my age, so I spent most nights watching TV with my grandparents.

One night, I was out walking by the boat docks. It was just me with the star-filled sky and lights shining off the water. I noticed one of the condo doors wide open and heard some noise. Being nosy, I walked over to see what was happening. Inside, I saw a father and son team doing construction work.

I stood there, dumbstruck, and said, "Hi, who are you guys?"

They introduced themselves and a mild flirtation began with the son. I appreciated a good-looking dude in a tool belt, so I would wait for their workday to start and casually walk by. Finally, the son got the hint and asked me on a date. I was so excited I could not stand it. My grandparents thought I was ridiculous. I got all ready one Friday night and waited and waited. He never showed up. I was heartbroken. I did not have his phone number because he said he would pick me up.

After pouting that night, the next day came and went, and there was a knock at the door. I answered it and it was him. I had the nights confused. I changed my clothes and was out the door before anyone could say no.

We went to see a concert by the Rossington Collins Band. They were the guys left of the group Lynyrd Skynyrd after the plane crash in 1977. Well, I had a blast. I do not know if he did or not, but I was crushing on him big time. I got home five minutes after curfew, and my grandfather was waiting at the door for us. He stood there in his underwear, T-shirt, and no teeth, yelling that I was late.

It sounds hilarious now, but then I was so embarrassed. I thought it was over before it began for my dream boy and me.

To my relief, that was not so. I had met my first true love. We got close quickly. He was going through a divorce from his first wife. He was the first friend I made, and I clung to him for dear life. I thought being clingy and needy was real love, but it was not.

Eventually, we moved in together. It was my first apartment and experience of living on my own. I remember it cost $250 per month. At first, it was fun—a lot of fun. Friends would come over on Friday night and not leave until Sunday night. He played guitar in a band and was a talented songwriter and musician. We went to a lot of outdoor venues and bar gigs. It was a party lifestyle. Drinking was a focal point of my life. I was not the only one in our group who blacked out and acted stupid. It was fairly common among the crowd.

It was easy to laugh it off in the beginning until the blackouts included physical fights, infidelity, and financial consequences. Of course, we would hide all these things from our families. He drank the same way I did, so that seemed okay to me. He got arrested a few times, and my logic was that he should quit drinking but not me because I had never been to jail.

I know now I wanted to fix him so that my life would be better. In hindsight, it was always about me somehow. The self-centeredness of my youth and my alcoholism was gaining a stronghold over my life and future. I could not imagine a life without partying. I thought it would be the most boring, empty life ever. This was a lie I told myself. I had zero self-worth and no self-respect because of all the stupid things I did. I had only the self-worth that anything or anyone outside of me said I did. I turned into a huge people pleaser.

The self-loathing was intense. I kept doing things that I knew were wrong, but I seemed to have no control over my behavior. That was another lie I told myself. As long as I could blame others for my problems, I justified my behavior.

I experienced a lot of love during those times from his family. Our families got to know each other and shared fantastic holidays together. Fun times that will never be forgotten, like Christmases up north in the snow and sing-alongs. All of the corny stuff our families did provided me with some of my best memories.

We broke up a few times and always managed to get back together. During one of the longer breakups, I moved back to Pennsylvania. My boyfriend and I had a massive fight after a drunken night. Considering my lack of thinking anything through and my knee-jerk reactions to life, it seemed like a good idea to rent a U-Haul and pack my stuff and go. So, I did. I was working as a medical assistant for a cardiologist, and I just abandoned him. I never got to make amends for that.

I had never pulled anything attached to a car before, so I was trying to pay attention to the road. My battery died in front of a 7-Eleven, sixty miles from home. I wondered if I should call my boyfriend and return, but decided no way that was happening. A mechanic from the garage next door installed a new battery and backed the car up so I could safely get on the road.

Like I said, I did not know how to drive with something hitched to my car. I made sure I only had to pull forward for the rest of the trip.

I stopped at a hotel that night in Georgia. It was the first time I had eaten alone in a restaurant, and it was an eerie feeling. Not one person in the world knew where I was. I called my mom from the hotel that night and told her I was coming home. She was excited until I said it was for good, not just a visit.

She was kind enough to let us use the revolving door policy. My sister Kelly lived in Virginia and was going to college at the time. My mother gave me the address, and I decided to visit her on my way home. There were no cell phones or GPS devices at that time, so I had to find my way.

When I left Florida, it was eighty-five degrees, and I was wearing a sundress. I had not considered any change in temperature or weather and froze when I arrived in Virginia. I took the wrong exit and ended up in a sketchy part of town. After calling her from a gas station, I finally made it to Kelly's apartment.

While driving north on the highway, I kept hearing two songs on the radio: Tina Turner's "Better Be Good to Me" and John Waite's "Missing You." I went from tears to anger and back again. Sentimental lyrics have done that to me over the years.

When I arrived at Kelly's apartment, she was adequately sympathetic toward me. I stayed a few days, then went home to my mom. Shortly after I arrived home, I was excited to hear Kelly was going to visit during her spring break. My youngest sister, Kolleen, was still living at home.

My mother had met a wonderful man and was trying to start a new life with him, and here I was, saying, "Hey, aren't you glad me and my boatload of issues are back?"

It was tons of fun being around my extended family again, but my drinking continued. I did not realize how much of a drinker Kelly was because we had not lived near each other in a few years. When we were younger, she was the good girl, saddled with keeping an eye on me, which was a lousy spot to be in. When we were kids, people asked us often if we were twins, and we started saying yes.

Kelly and I decided to go out drinking one night. Nothing crazy, just to a restaurant called Chi-Chi's. For some reason, we took Kolleen's car. When we left Chi-Chi's, we were a little tipsy and kept laughing at everything. We decided to keep partying and stopped at one of the local corner bars. Well, we had one, I repeat *one* drink there, and the night went crazy.

The next thing I remember, we were stuck in a field in Kolleen's car. Kelly was behind the wheel, and the car would not move. We got in a huge fight because she would not let me try to drive the car out of there. I got out of the passenger seat, walked around the car, and grabbed her out of the driver seat.

During our scuffle, her ear got cut and bled all over my jacket and on her shirt.

The next thing we saw were blue lights coming toward us. As the police pulled up to us, all of a sudden, I realized Kelly was gone!

They asked me what happened and why there was blood on me.

"You have to find my sister," I kept repeating. "She disappeared."

I was very combative when drunk, and that night was no different. I ended up fighting them, but, of course, they won. I was hog-tied, thrown into the back of the police cruiser, and taken to jail. After I was processed, they called my house because I kept asking about my sister.

Mom verified my story. She also told them Kelly had gotten home safe, and I was relieved.

Mom was relieved—and mad—to learn that I was safe in custody. The story Kelly had given Mom was that a kind man and his son gave her a ride home. She'd told Mom she didn't know what had happened to me, and Mom had been distraught until the police had phoned.

Now she was just furious. She and Jerry got me out of jail and brought me home.

I knew she was disgusted with me. What could I say? I had no defense.

When we got home, I crawled into bed with Kelly. We concluded that someone had roofied our drinks at the second bar—Rohypnol, known as "roofies," was the date rape drug of the 1980s—because that amount of alcohol had never made us so delirious. We'd only had one drink at the second bar before completely losing it—and we knew we were both better drinkers than that!

The next morning, Mom opened the door and saw us laughing and giggling about everything.

"You two make me sick," she said and slammed the door.

That made us laugh even harder. It has always been like that between us. We could scream and fight but five minutes later be crying and apologizing to each other. I have always adored my sisters. Without them, there would be no me.

Kelly went back to school the next week, and eventually I had to pay a fine. We were in significant trouble for wrecking my little sister's car. She was so mad at us. I don't remember if it got fixed or not.

Looking back, these seem like relatively innocent stories of trouble. But my episodes got more dangerous and scarier as time went by.

Kelly, on the other hand, seemed to be on a better path. We were all very proud of Kelly. She was the only one who was going college. I knew my mom and dad helped with expenses, but she paid for most of the tuition on her own.

I always admired that drive for her education, but if I were 100 percent honest, I would say I was also jealous. I have always been smart but not formally educated. I blew my opportunity for school. I am envious of people today with a formal education. Drinking and drugs were more important—so no degree for me.

When Kelly was about to graduate from college, Mom, Kendra, Kolleen, and I made plans to drive to Richmond, Virginia, for the celebration and ceremony. Mom wanted us to ride together, but Kendra and I came up with a lame excuse to ride separately. We wanted to drink on the way and knew Mom would not be down with that. Against her better judgment, Mom said okay, and she and Kolleen left together.

Kendra and I managed to get on the road a few hours later. We wanted to be there in time for the big party that night at Kelly's house, and it was about a six-hour drive.

About two hours in, we saw a bar on the side of the highway somewhere in Maryland. We decided to stop for a little early refreshment.

It was like walking into a different era. It was midday on Friday. The bar was dark inside and smelled nasty. We looked at each other with that silent communication of sisters, then walked up to the bar and ordered our drinks. There were only six other people in there, and they were all men. They seemed like good ole country boys. We liked meeting new people and would drink with almost anyone.

A song came on the jukebox. Suddenly Fred "August" Campbell was crooning something about all your friends are assholes, and you are an asshole too. We had never heard this song before, and we laughed so hard we were crying. After a few drinks and replays of our new favorite lyrics, we paid our tab and continued on our way.

Near Baltimore, my car started to buck and sputter. Thankfully, there was a Ford dealership just ahead. I paid for a new belt with a check I knew would bounce, and we continued the drive to Richmond.

Near Alexandria, where we used to live when we were younger, the car started to smoke and sputter again! I pulled over to the shoulder of the highway as the engine seized. We were so close but still so far.

We realized at that point that going against Mom's intuition was not too bright. Now it was raining, and we were stranded. We started walking in the rain and decided to hitchhike to Alexandria and get a tow truck.

So there we were, two girls in their twenties, wearing shorts, T-shirts, and flip-flops, walking in the rain down the highway. A semi-trailer truck pulled over and offered us a ride. We said yes, and Kendra sat behind the driver with a shoe in her hand, ready to clobber him if he tried any funny business. It was hysterical.

We finally got to a gas station and asked the manager about a tow truck. He laughed at us and said no way he was sending a tow truck on that highway during rush hour on a Friday.

My father and his second wife lived not too far away in a fancy area called Old Town. We didn't want to have to call Dad to ask for help, so we tried many ways to get out of this mess. Eventually we had no choice but to call Dad. We ended up taking one of his cars to Richmond and finally arrived that night. The party had started, and we had some serious catching up to do. Mom was relieved we made it safely to Kelly's house, and we were too!

We were so proud of Kelly getting her degree and watching her graduate the next day. I give my dad props for that incident because he took care of getting my car towed and fixed. Come to find out, he had a friend who owned a garage. All ended well that time. The I-95 "asshole" song gained new fans after that day.

7

California, Here I Come

KELLY SPEAKS

After college, I had gotten a full-time job teaching at a long-term residential treatment center for troubled teens. The center followed a positive peer culture model (PPC), founded by Harry Vorrath. The premise was that troubled teens develop self-worth, significance, dignity, and responsibility through commitment to the positive values of helping and caring for others.

My new students and I participated in climbing walls, ropes courses, backpacking trips, and rock climbing. I learned the value of building relationships through physical challenges and outdoor activities.

I taught an all-girls adolescent group and had a self-contained classroom. This meant that I taught all high school curriculum from grades nine through twelve. Flexibility was my middle name because I adapted to serious incidences and daily crisis.

If one of the girls refused to get out of bed and come to school, we would have school on the cottage. If one of the girls got violent, flipped over a desk, or punched a fist through a window, we would restrain her and have an impromptu group after she calmed down. These girls were bright but underachieving. They all were trauma survivors.

Truth be told, I was closer to the students' age than most of the staff. One time, a probation officer came onto campus and thought I was a student. He asked me where he could find the teacher. After that, I started wearing conservative and frumpy clothing, such as flannel skirts, to appear more mature than I was.

Teachers were expected to attend the girls' daily group therapy sessions with the psychologist. Our team included licensed therapists, psychiatrists, teachers, residential line staff, recreational therapists, and ancillary services. Even the office manager attended the multidisciplinary team meetings.

I loved the kids and was able to support them and "hold space" for them. I provided safety and nurturing, without judgement, to give them room to address their trauma. The kids demonstrated so much courage. They had enormous strength and undiscovered talent. I was honored to be a part of their team. This professional and personal experience would change my life.

The director of the facility was tall in stature, wore cowboy boots, had a beard, and was considered a rebel by the staff and students. He commanded respect from all of us. Most important, though, was that he mentored me and taught me valuable skills.

I was being paid to create a nurturing and loving environment for students, in a place where my talents were developed by professionals who saw something in me beyond what I could see in myself. I considered this divine intervention, and to this day I am eternally grateful for the experience.

We had a tight group of staff that worked hard at the facility and partied hard on the weekends. Staff trainings were intense, and we were expected to take risks. This created a certain amount of vulnerability, and occasionally my trauma was triggered.

One day, a colleague took me aside after a team meeting. "Tell me about your family," she said. No one else was around; it was just the two of us. She was standing in front of a whiteboard.

I was surprised by the question.

"Tell me about your parents and grandparents," she urged. "Describe their personalities, strengths, and challenges."

As I answered, she began drawing a picture. Then she asked questions about my sisters, birth order, and other history detailing different attributes of close and extended relatives. She was drawing a Genogram.

I was immediately intrigued.

I didn't know at the time what this was, but my whole world opened up. Right in front of me in a diagram, I was able to see my family's multigenerational patterns. I visually saw the role alcoholism and mental illness had played with previous generations. I saw the roles that my sisters and I played to cope with my father's alcoholism and abuse.

After interviewing me and evaluating all the data I gave her, she explained that I was "an adult child of an alcoholic." She asked me to evaluate my relationships with my sisters. She educated me about the roles of family members and siblings who grew up in alcoholic homes.

My role was "The Hero." I was an overachiever, extremely responsible, perfectionistic, and a Type A personality.

Karen was the "Scapegoat." She was blamed for the family's problems and an alcoholic/addict.

Kendra and Kolleen had characteristics of "The Lost Child" and "The Mascot." They would use humor to diffuse stressful situations. They blended into the woodwork and didn't create a lot of problems.

Eureka! This was an aha moment.

There was relief in being able to put structure to my family's dysfunction. It was like solving a puzzle. I would study Claudia Black's work for years. (claudiablack.com) I also began attending Adult Children of Alcoholics (ACA) meetings.

Another author who had a tremendous influence on me was Robin Norwood. She wrote a book called *Women Who Love Too Much*. The book identified how women repeat unhealthy patterns in relationships with men. I saw my sister's and my choices in relationships through a new lens after reading the book.

In addition to attending ACA meetings, I began outpatient therapy sessions. I feel blessed that I'm a seeker. I wanted to understand the whys. I tried to make sense of the abuse and trauma I suffered and desired to heal memories of past violent episodes. I wanted to avoid repeating patterns of behavior from my parents or previous generations. I wanted to make different choices. I wanted to let go of the deep resentment and feelings of abandonment I had about my father.

I wanted to be free.

By then, my father had divorced his second wife, moved to California, and was dating a woman who would soon become his third wife. He invited me to visit him, and I was excited about the opportunity to reconnect.

Participating in Adult Children of Alcoholics and individual counseling, I started to develop empathy for what it must have been like for my parents. After all, they had four children by the age of twenty-four with all the attendant pressures and responsibilities.

During my visit, my dad had set me up with a younger colleague who volunteered to take me sightseeing. We got lost and drunk that day; however, I saw the ocean, mountains, and desert all in twenty-four hours. Huntington Beach, Big Bear, and Palm Springs were magnificent. I fell in love with the beauty and different terrains of California.

Before I returned to Virginia, Dad gave me an invitation that shocked me.

"Hey Kel," he said, "Why don't you consider moving here? To California?"

"Really?"

"You can live in my condo rent free."

"Really?"

"I'm moving in with my fiancé. She has a great home on the beach in Sunset."

"Really?

"Sure, it will be nice to have my daughter living close by."

How could I say no? I was ecstatic. I returned home with my resignation letter in hand.

But that week at work, my mentor was not thrilled at the news.

"This probably won't work out the way you're hoping, Kelly," he said frankly.

"What do you mean?"

"You are chasing a fantasy. You want something from your dad he's not capable of giving."

"Don't you think I should at least try?"

"I'm afraid he's going to hurt you, maybe even crush your heart."

He would be right, but it was all part of my journey. I took his counsel under advisement, but it was my lesson to learn, and I was willing to take the risk.

It was difficult to leave my job and the relationships I had established. The goodbyes to my students were especially tough. They put a play together for me as a surprise and sang "Hotel California" by the Eagles as a parting gift. It was a touching gesture and one that I still remember.

My friends from college threw me a going-away party. When I walked into the party, there was a Depends package of adult diapers on top of the TV as a going-away present. As previously noted, when I was drunk, I often peed my pants. It was all in good fun. We all laughed and thought it was hilarious. Another mentor who was a teacher at the residential facility and a good friend helped me pack up my belongings and drove cross country with me. We had a great time camping and sightseeing.

My relationship with Dad started out great. He was attentive, and I enjoyed one-on-one time with him, which I never got as a kid.

To help us connect and have some shared experiences, I jumped into some of the hobbies and interests he enjoyed. I got my PADI scuba diving certificate, began running, and enjoyed beach time with him.

It looked so good on the surface that a friend of mine couldn't believe the stories I told him about my childhood experiences and Dad's abuse. My friend said that in observing the two of us, he would give us the father-daughter award.

Our relationship was fun for a couple of years until I disagreed with him about something and he disowned me.

After a visit with my sisters, he had been encouraging Kolleen to be as promiscuous as possible. She was my baby sister, impressionable and young, and I was furious. I told him how inappropriate it was to give this kind of advice to Kolleen.

He left me a vicious voice mail, telling me he didn't want to hear any of my psychobabble bullshit, demanding to know who was I to tell him how to behave.

I kept the abusive and attacking voice mail message and played it for my friend.

I said, "Meet my father!"

I was twenty-four years old, and the year was 1987. I got a job teaching special education with a public school district in Santa Ana, California, at a middle school. I taught in a self-contained classroom, and my students had a variety of learning differences.

The special education classrooms were located in the back of the property in a trailer. Some teachers and staff thought we had it easy because we had reduced classroom sizes, classroom aides, and less transition during the day. Someone warned me that some of the traditional classroom teachers shunned the special education teachers in the lounge. I thought this was absurd until I experienced it.

One day, the principal called me into his office and spoke to me as if I were a slow learner. He explained that some of my students were complaining that I was giving them homework. He said that, given the disabilities of my students, perhaps remembering to do homework was too much. He thought it best that I eliminate homework moving forward.

I could not believe the level of intolerance and ignorance from the administration and teachers toward my students.

I've always had a heart for the underdog, and as far as I was concerned, his words were fightin' words. I determined to find a way to encourage my students' strengths, build confidence in their learning styles, and increase their exposure on campus.

I joined forces with the resource special education teacher, and we developed a friendship. I kept my head down and worked behind the scenes to help my students thrive in the classroom.

My teacher's aide was bilingual and spoke fluent Spanish as well as English. She was my right hand, and we worked well together. Of course, I quickly learned the essential cuss words from my students, who thought I was unaware of what they were saying!

Santa Ana, California, was 80 percent Hispanic at that time, and I enjoyed learning about my students' home environments, culture, and challenges. Many came from modest to low-income neighborhoods and shared apartments or homes with relatives. Many were hard-working immigrants who worked long hours to provide for their families.

I learned that students perform to the level of expectation that adults around them set. My expectations of them were high. And, of course, I continued giving homework.

Mrs. Burd Becomes Californian

MS. BURD AND

Ms. Kelly Ann Burd lives in Huntington Beach. Ms. Burd teaches reading, spelling, science, English, and math at Sierra Intermediate School in Trailor 2. Ms. Kelly Ann Burd taught in Richmond, Virginia. She taught at a private school called Charterhouse, grades 9-11.

Ms. Kelly Ann Burd enjoys teaching and enjoying working with young people. Ms. Burd's favorite subjects are English and science. Her classroom rules are to respect others, be on time, and be prepared with paper and pencil, and no eating.

Ms. Burd has many hobbies and interests. Ms. Burd loves pizza. She says she could eat it every night. She enjoys reading all kinds of books. She is going to college at night, and reads a lot. Her favorite TV show is "Head Of The Class." She loves all kinds of music; jazz, rock, and soft music. She enjoys all kinds of sports. For example, bicycling, playing baseball, football, jogging, and doing aerobics.

Ms. Burd had an interesting journey. She traveled across the country when she moved from Richmond, Virginia, to California. She saw Virginia, North Carolina, South Carolina, Tennesses, Arkansas, Texas, New Mexico, Arizona, Colorado, and California. She also lived in Illinois, Pennsylvania, and New Jersey. Ms. Burd is happy that she moved and is enjoying her first year at Sierra. She has a great class.

I implemented a token economy system where the students earned raffle tickets for positive behavior and performance. Every Friday, they could exchange the tickets at our store, stocked with various products: school supplies, art supplies, and candy.

I also created incentives for the kids to earn off-campus field trips. My boys wanted to go to an Angel's baseball game at Anaheim Stadium. My girls wanted to go rollerblading at Balboa Island, then back to my apartment to make dinner and enjoy ice cream and cake. I decided it would cost 450 raffle tickets. No one thought that the students could delay gratification long enough to earn these field trips. I knew they could. It took months to save the tickets, but they did, and boy did we have fun!

Another assignment I gave my students was to interview other teachers on campus to learn about their hobbies and interests. Their articles were published in the school newspaper. My students enjoyed the assignment, and we were successful in building their value and confidence at school.

I felt fulfilled. I had a full-time job that I loved, and I was enjoying all the wonderful, new experiences California had to offer. I felt my drinking was under control (and whenever I compared my drinking to my dad's, it further convinced me I didn't have a problem at all!).

I had zero desire to date, get married, or have kids. It was vital for me to be financially independent and to blaze my own trail.

Then, I met Bob.

8

Karen Takes the Scenic Route

KAREN SPEAKS

Jerry had been offered a great job opportunity in Dallas, Texas. This meant he would have to leave the security of his vested position at the Lehigh Valley Airport. Mom and Jerry decided to take a chance on a new life and move to Dallas. I was proud of them for taking this risk.

Because I had no place to go once they left, they were gracious enough to let me move with them. While I was thankful to spend this time with my mom, I felt like the third wheel and thought they should have their space and privacy.

On top of that, it didn't take me long to realize I wasn't a Texas girl.

About that time, I received a phone call from my ex-boyfriend's mother in Florida. I could tell by her tone she was very upset.

"Karen, I'm calling to let you know my son has been admitted into the hospital and is in the ICU unit. If you want to see him, you need to come soon."

"What happened?"

"All I know is he was ambushed by a man and his son when he went to collect a lousy forty-dollar debt."

"That's horrible!"

"They beat him senseless with a lead pipe. He has a brain injury and may not recover."

After a few days, his condition did improve, and I was able to talk to him directly. We continued talking over the next few weeks as he recovered. I realized I was still in love with him.

I was awestruck when he said, "Karen, I've never stopped loving you. Why don't you come back? I'll come get you, baby, and bring you home."

Riding in the car with him back to Florida felt like the most natural thing. On the drive back he told me, "It doesn't seem like we have been apart for over a year."

"I know," I said with a sigh. "I've really missed you."

I came to find out later the beating he received had been from a jealous husband. The drinking and drugging continued. We had been together off and on for eight years. We thought getting married was the next logical step in our relationship. The fact that we were both alcoholics and drug addicts didn't seem to be a concern at all.

What could possibly go wrong?

I found a job at a family-owned dental supply company. I loved the job, and the people I worked for were great to me. They paid me well and gave me bonuses. They were guests at my wedding and generous with their gifts. I respected all of them and had met their wives and children.

Then I was invited to a housewarming party at one of their homes. I got drunk and made such a fool of myself that I got fired on Monday morning. My boss felt bad firing me, but his wife insisted. Why? At the party, I had made a pass at her husband and told him if he ever got tired of his wife, I would be willing to take her place. I lied to my husband about why I was fired and prayed that he would never find out the truth.

I was always appalled at my behavior after I sobered up.

But the truth was that my moral barometer was sinking lower and lower.

After six months, my husband and I got divorced. You see, he had quit drinking, and I could not. This was the first time I paid a consequence that really hurt. The car wrecks and humiliations hadn't phased me, but getting divorced broke my heart. It was not out of the blue, that is for sure. I had many chances to stop drinking. I just could not.

One day, my grandfather called me and told me to be ready at seven o'clock that night because he was picking me up for real estate classes. Pops had already paid for the materials, so I could not say no.

We went to the classes for about three months, two nights a week. It was fun. Pops, who loved attention, was the class clown. I passed the class with flying colors. He flunked because he was buzzed most of the time. But he didn't care; he said he only signed us both up for the classes to be sure I would go.

I envisioned selling beautiful mansions on the glittering waters of the Intracoastal Waterway in Fort Lauderdale. What I ended up doing was selling timeshare apartments on the beach. It was a close second. I'd never had a job that was based on straight commission before, so I was nervous that I would be a big failure. Well, I was not. I found out I had a gift for gab, inherited from my dad.

When I started selling timeshares, I was thrilled that I hadn't had a drink in two months.

Then I saw the patio bar.

My new place of employment was an alcoholics' paradise. It seemed that everyone who worked there partied hard. It was too perfect.

Despite drinking again, I started to gain self-confidence in the job department. I also did not stay single for long. I got myself into a rebound relationship. He was a manager at work, so I could call in hungover whenever I wanted. It was awesome. And it didn't hurt that he drank as much as I did.

I had arrived!

One night, we were all going out after work to celebrate the twenty-first birthday of a coworker. Two bars, Dirty Nellie's and Shooters, had boat docks up and down the Intracoastal. You could walk back and forth from one bar to the next on the boat docks.

The night started great as usual, and it was a lot of fun. I picked a fight with my boyfriend, which was par for the course when I was drinking. I ditched him and walked out of that bar into another.

When morning rolled around, I couldn't figure out where I was and whose bed I was in. This was typical blackout behavior for me. My car was still at the bar, so my "new friend" gave me a ride back. Apparently, we had ridden to his place on a motorcycle.

I had zero recollection of the motorcycle ride. This scared me. I could have fallen off the bike, gotten messed up—or worse, died! I have met people over the years who have done prison time for their actions during a blackout.

When I was young, I learned from my dad that there's always a price to pay for bad behavior. I got used to paying consequences. I understood that if I wanted to dance, I'd have to pay the fiddler.

But the consequences kept getting scarier and scarier.

After that experience, I stayed home from work for an entire week out of shame and humiliation. I was desperate for a solution to my drinking problem. I didn't know where to turn. I had been to a few twelve-step meetings in my mid-twenties and wrote them off because their goal was sobriety. At that time of my life, I could not fathom never drinking again.

And why should I? I wasn't an old man living under a bridge. I wasn't homeless or jobless. Besides, if I quit drinking, what would I do for fun? Would I even have any friends left?

The truth was, I didn't want to stop. I still wanted to drink, just not make a complete idiot out of myself. I wanted to learn to drink like a lady. I also thought I should be able to make these changes on my own. I felt successful in other aspects of my life, so why should this be different? I considered myself a complete moral failure and hated myself for that weakness. I could not stop.

When I starting hearing about people getting hypnotized to quit smoking, I was intrigued. I figured if it worked for smoking, maybe it would work for drinking. That sounded great to me. Someone else could perform this miracle. They would do the work, and I would sit in a comfortable chair. They could wave the magic wand and—voila!—I would be sober.

I made an appointment with a hypnotist named "Mr. Right." Of course, I thought that was hysterical. When I went to my first appointment, I told him I had been looking for him for a very long time. I cracked myself up. (Like he'd never heard that one before, right?)

After five sessions, I was shocked when my obsession with alcohol seemed removed. It was the first of many divine interventions I experienced in my life. Immediately, my life greatly improved. I gained expertise at my job, got promoted a few times, and earned the respect of my peers and myself. My family started to view me differently. They were finally proud of me!

It felt terrific. I could look at myself in the mirror and not despise my reflection. I owned my own home and was making serious money. I had lots of friends and was still living with rebound man. My life looked great from the outside.

So why was I miserable? What did it mean to be happy? Was this it? I just could not accept that this was all life had for me.

I started to seek answers from shrinks and psychologists. I was becoming convinced there was something inherently wrong with me. I thought I was a bad seed. Many years later, I came to understand that I was beyond any human help.

In the meantime, I buried myself under layers and layers of justification and rationalization. *If other people had my childhood, they would feel like this too*, I told myself. Self-pity and arrogance were my companions. I was what is called a dry drunk—restless, irritable, and discontent.

My only solace was work and keeping busy. We opened at 7:00 a.m. and worked till after the last customer left, sometimes as late as 10:00 p.m. I spent sixteen years working with this company and was proud of that. Work was the only part of my life that gave me any self-esteem.

Then the unthinkable happened. Pops got lung cancer. Anyone who has watched a loved one die from this disease knows how painful it is. I tried to help my grandmother as much as possible. In the process, I started using some prescribed medicine for anxiety and depression. I would make myself a cocktail of pills to chill out. It seemed innocent enough to me.

After Pops died, I tried to return to everyday life but didn't know how to process my grief or my feelings. I just learned how to stuff everything and tell everyone I was okay. I was conditioned to live with a high level of emotional pain. I always said I would rather take a physical beating than have someone mess with my head. Somehow, that option seemed easier.

I continued taking prescribed medication for anxiety and depression—along with street drugs. Think about it! No smell, no wrecked cars, no blackouts, no going home with strangers. No one seemed to know, so why not?

My thirties were coming to an end. Time was ticking by, and it was too late for me to have children, so I squashed any desire for a family of my own. In life we grieve things we wanted and never had. We grieve people, lost opportunities, even unfulfilled dreams and fantasies. I did not think a loving relationship would be part of my future, and I grieved that too.

My workplace was my central social hub. Turnover of employees was high, and I met hundreds of salespeople over the years. One day I noticed a new salesman. The first time I saw him, I knew somewhere inside of me that I was going to be with him. He was the best-looking man I had ever seen, including movie stars. It was lust at first sight. I watched him and made sure I was in his path at every opportunity.

When we all went to happy hour, I noticed that he drank Diet Coke—just like me! I began to think we would be perfect for each other. After all, the only people who don't drink alcohol at happy hours are alcoholics. Ironic but true. That's all the criteria I needed. I had the childish belief that if we were together, life would be peaches and cream.

He knew I was giddy over him. I experienced butterflies in my stomach for the first time in twenty years. Oh, I was in trouble. The only problem was that I was still living with rebound man in a home we owned together.

When I left that relationship, it felt intoxicating. Wow, new hope, new love. What a feeling! I was finally getting my shot at happiness. I was over the moon.

We moved in together quickly. Even though I should have known better, I ignored a number of red flags. I told myself that his controlling ways meant he loved me and wanted to watch out for me.

He was 100 percent honest with me about his alcoholic past. He had been to the bottom of the heap and was working his way out. None of these things mattered to me. I had my own source of income, so I did not care about his financial means. I took a lot of flak at work about my new relationship, but again, I did not care. My boss told me that people were gossiping about us. So what? They thought they were perfect? I didn't care about that either.

The first four months of our relationship were great. We were making a lot of money. We ate fancy dinners out and isolated from the rest of the world.

One day I started to notice a change in his attitude. Then I began to notice a slight smell of liquor emitting from his skin at night. I was too afraid to confront him. I thought he would leave me. If that happened, I felt my life would be over. It took me years to understand what codependency was, but apparently, I was the epitome of codependency.

He finally confessed that he was drinking again.

I said I knew because I could smell the liquor coming out of his pores.

It took me years to learn that if I were powerless over my alcoholism, how could I possibly have power over someone else's? Soon after that, he quit working, and life changed for us. I thought I knew what alcoholism was. After all, I had spent my life around alcoholics, including my dad, boyfriends, other family members, and myself.

But this was different.

He started drinking around the clock. He drank two huge bottles of vodka a day. I was petrified. I thought for sure he was going to die. My family told me to get out. So did his friends. So did my friends. No one suggested I stick it out. After all, we had been together for less than a year.

But I felt it was my duty to help him and save him. I thought I had been discarded as damaged goods in my life and swore to myself I would never do that to someone I loved. I was living a grown-up's life with a child's belief system. I did not understand that I was living in a fantasy world, unaware of what reality was. It took another twelve years for me to learn that I had no foundation or skill set to manage my problems.

He told me not to tell anyone about his drinking. This demand seemed normal to me because I was conditioned to keep alcoholic secrets. Oh God, there I went, keeping secrets again.

I never knew what to expect when I came home from work, but this was not an unfamiliar experience. I did not want to re-live the terrorism of my childhood, and I was frantic. Sometimes I would lay in a ball on the floor, crying and thinking that I had left this part of my life behind me.

I had no common sense and was completely ill-equipped to handle this situation. I started using more potent opiates. That worked temporarily.

My ten-year love affair with opiates had begun, and I never saw it coming. It crept up on me quietly and softly, then slowly took over my entire life. I became Superwoman on opiates. I had all kinds of energy to work lots of hours, take care of my home, and I felt great. I thought I had found my answer. This must be what normal people felt like.

I had enough money to stay supplied with all the drugs I needed. In the early 2000s, pill mills were popping up all over South Florida. All you needed was an X-ray and you could walk out of your appointment with bags of drugs. These "doctors" owned their own pharmacies and filled scripts on-site.

Part of me hated those places and the people that oper-ated them. I knew they were criminals and lacked any con-science, giving out scripts knowing they were making junkies out of many innocent people who had real pain.

I, however, wasn't one of those people. I wasn't innocent. I wasn't in physical pain. My goal was to stay high. And it was easy to do. This was before the state established any regula-tions. People went to three or four doctors to get drugs, com-monly known as doctor shopping. I became immersed in a sub-culture consumed with buying, selling, and trading drugs.

Even I could see where this was heading. And, indeed, that's where we've gone. The entire country has seen the explosion of a horrifying opiate epidemic in the last twenty years.

My moral compass kept getting lower. It was evident at my job that I no longer held myself to any performance standard. I got so high at work my friends would take me home to protect me from being disciplined. It was unspoken knowledge that I had turned into a real-life junkie.

My boyfriend had started using drugs with me—and I was cool with that because at least he wasn't drinking anymore. But we sank deeper and deeper into the abyss of addiction. No matter how many drugs we had, it was never enough.

We started buying heroin off the street when the pharmaceuticals ran out. But I never saw myself as a drug addict. Weren't drug addicts unemployed and living on the street? Didn't they steal from old ladies? I wasn't that bad . . . yet. I was still better than them in my mind.

At one point, I took family leave allowed by law to get myself together. I had pure intentions at the beginning, then happily discovered that I could get high all the time with this time off.

One day it dawned on me that I was no longer sober.

Can you believe this? I had been using hard drugs for three years straight, and I still thought I was sober because I had not consumed alcohol. Oh, how strong denial can be!

I decided to check myself into a detox unit. That was probably the first right decision I made in years. My boyfriend insisted he could detox himself alone at home. He said he was an expert at this.

I only stayed at the detox unit one night. The next morning, I had a bad feeling, checked myself out, and drove home.

When I got there, I discovered my boyfriend had drunk so much and taken so many pills he was having seizures. After a violent fight, I called 911. My boyfriend was taken by ambulance to the hospital, and Baker Acted. That means he was held against his will because he was a danger to himself.

I was forty years old, mentally distraught and physically ill from the withdrawals. I couldn't think straight. I called my mom, then living in Texas with Jerry. When she asked me if I wanted her to come down, I cried and begged, "Yes, please."

I was crying and babbling and not making much sense.

She and my stepdad got on the next plane to help me. They did not hesitate to come and waited till they arrived to ask any questions. I will never forget that.

In the meantime, there was a knock at my front door. On her way to the airport, Mom had called Kelly's mother-in-law, Pat, who lived close to me. She asked her to take me to her house. As we left my house, I looked back at the shattered glass and destruction laying all around.

She showed me kindness, and I loved her for it. That afternoon, she went to the airport to pick up my mother and Jerry. When they arrived back at the house, Mom and Jerry were shocked at what they saw. I was super skinny and extremely sick. I was going through the worst part of withdrawals. This meant I was sweating, nauseous, shaking, had chills, and could not think straight. I felt like I could die. I kept whining about my boyfriend, and they told me he was safe in the hospital.

Since I asked them to come, they probably thought I was ready for real help. But I still only wanted to do things "my way."

When I told my parents I was not returning to Texas with them for inpatient treatment, they were angry and confused.

"Why did you call us if you're not willing to accept help?" my mother asked.

And it was an excellent question.

My body and brain were way off-kilter. I did not believe I could ever restore my natural capabilities. I thought I would be left brain damaged forever.

My family went back to Texas, and my boyfriend came home from the hospital. We did not want to break up, but we were both sick and incapable of any type of real love.

I found an intensive outpatient rehab forty miles from my home and, for six weeks, managed to drive forty miles every day to treatment. When therapists suggested I also attend AA meetings, I refused. I figured if I was at the rehab center all day, what good would another meeting do?

I never went back to my job. I knew I would use drugs there. After sixteen years of high-pressure sales and repetition in my career, I resigned. I had a feeling I was going to be fired anyway.

My boyfriend and I came up with a great plan to buy a motorhome and race car, then travel the country as racers. You can see what a sane and balanced decision this was. Quickly, our plan fell apart and we were devastated. It was the right timing for a fresh start. On a vacation with my boyfriend to Daytona Beach, I fell in love with a little town named DeLand, whose population is a mere thirty thousand. Deland is twenty-five miles west of Daytona Beach. It seemed like Mayberry RFD to me.

How could I get into trouble in such an innocent small town?

I was about to find out.

KELLY SPEAKS

When Karen lived in Boca Raton, I was proud of her. I thought she had been sober for ten years and was building a good life. She owned her own home and had a successful career. I did not realize she was using other substances, which would soon lead to complete destruction.

When things began to unravel, I was embarrassed that my mother-in-law had gotten an up-close-and-personal view of our family dysfunction.

We were concerned about her dependency and obsession with her new boyfriend. The family began to realize and witness the downward spiral Karen's life was taking.

9

Romance Is in the Air

KELLY SPEAKS

I was meeting my dad and his third wife for dinner at Chili's, and they were late. As I waited at the bar for them to arrive, the bartender, a woman, started making small talk.

Eventually, she said, "Hey, girl, I think you got stood up."

I responded, "I hope not; it's my father."

Little did I know that I'd caught the eye of the restaurant manager, Bob, who had asked the bartender to find out more about me. After she told him I was waiting for my father and not a date, he came by our table frequently throughout the evening, "checking in" to make sure the three of us were happy with our meals.

He was tall, lean, and wore braces. I thought he was a little geeky and overly enthusiastic. It was clear he was enamored with me, and my stepmother teased me about it.

Toward the end of dinner, Bob gave me a business card for complimentary dinners for two and invited me to come back soon.

Embarrassed by his attention, I left the restaurant quickly. But Dad and my stepmother kept badgering me to call Bob.

After a couple of weeks, I dialed his phone number.

"Hi," I said awkwardly when he answered. "I don't know if you remember me, but this is Kelly."

"Of course, I do," he said warmly. "I'm so happy you called. You didn't leave your phone number on the credit card receipt."

By our fourth date, I knew I wanted to marry him. He would tell me later that when I walked into Chili's that night, he told his staff he was going to marry me!

We had so much in common. As children, both of our families moved around a lot. By coincidence, our fathers knew each other through the restaurant industry and traveled in some of the same circles. Two of our sisters had troubled pasts. We shared the same values of family, hard work, faith, and fun.

Because I worked at the school from 7:00 a.m. till 3:00 p.m. and Bob closed the restaurant at 1:00 a.m., our schedules were difficult to coordinate. But Bob supported my teaching and participated in some of the outings I did with my students.

One day I took my kids on a field trip from Santa Ana to Huntington Beach. I had been shocked to learn that many of the students did not travel outside of their barrios and had never seen the beach, which was only thirty minutes away. On our way to the beach, Bob opened Chili's early and made everyone burgers, fries, and sodas for free. We were the only customers in the restaurant! Their mouths could not open wide enough to fit the burgers in. My students were in hog heaven!

It was clear to me that Bob had a big heart and a generous nature.

When two of my boys had earned the 450 raffle tickets for a field trip to an Angels baseball game, their parents gave permission for Bob to go with us. My kids were delighted! Bob bought them every souvenir possible, in addition to all the junk food available. We had hot dogs, cotton candy, peanuts, and hot pretzels. I would not be surprised if the kids got sick when they got home. I don't think it mattered; it only added to the adventure.

Before the end of the game, we snuck closer to the field. (I know this wasn't the best role modeling, but we were living in the moment.) Well, we got on the jumbotron. There we were on the big screen! What a way to end the memorable night.

Margaritas, Anyone?

I do not want to glamorize my drinking. I don't want to minimize my alcoholism. For me, there was a fine line between alcohol use, alcohol abuse, and full-fledged alcoholism. My alcoholism took years to materialize. Partying was fun for many years until it wasn't.

My mid-twenties in Southern California were fantastic. I lived a mile from the beach. I was in great physical shape. I biked, rollerbladed, and ran 5Ks. I worked hard and played hard. Since Bob was the Manager at Chili's, my friends and I often enjoyed free margaritas.

Chili's builds an incredible culture with their employees, and I participated in Chili cook-offs and parties. I was particularly excited when Bob invited me to a wine-tasting event. I knew it would be a "sophisticated and formal" evening, and I looked forward to the opportunity to dress up.

That night, I learned that when you taste wine, you are supposed to swirl it around in your mouth and spit it out into a spittoon. I was surprised! Who does that? Who would waste the wine and the buzz? Not me.

I couldn't bring myself to spit the wine out. I got drunk and was hungover the next morning. This would become a memorialized event that was written off as a joke and affectionately called "The Wine Tasting Contest."

It wasn't the only drunken episode that would be minimized and laughed off.

When my sisters came out to visit, we celebrated by driving to Palm Springs for dinner. We had platters and plates piled high, and it was getting in the way of my drinking. I had one too many margaritas, and when the waiter asked if we were finished with our dinners, I yelled, "Take it away, Gus!" The other patrons stopped and stared at me. To this day, my sisters and I still holler, "Take it away, Gus!" and have a good laugh.

One New Year's Eve, when I was so drunk I didn't think I could make it to the bathroom to throw up, I yelled "Bucket! Bucket!" to my mom and Bob. I had inadvertently coined another phrase that would become part of our family lore.

Incidents like these became family jokes. These individual occurrences were explained away. After all, my drunken behavior was nowhere near as severe as Karen's. I might get loud, rude, and obnoxious, but I never rolled cars or ended up in jail.

Karen's outrageous behavior allowed me to justify and minimize mine.

After four months of dating, Bob asked me if I wanted to go looking at diamond rings. He hadn't proposed yet but said he wanted to know what type of rings I liked. You can imagine my level of excitement! We went to the mall and visited jewelry stores, learning about the cut, clarity, color, and size of diamonds.

My level of enthusiasm, however, waned when the sales associate asked about our wedding date. Bob's intentions were pure, but I realized this shopping excursion was premature.

I suggested we put any future shopping on hold until he was ready to formally pop the question.

One night a few months later, Bob invited me to dinner and told me to dress up. He was secretive and wouldn't give me any other details other than to meet him at Tony Roma's, the place where we'd had our first date.

As we were having a drink, the manager walked up and addressed Bob.

"Your transportation has arrived," he said warmly.

Outside, a black stretch limousine awaited us. Imagine my surprise!

"What's this for?" I queried.

"To take us to the beach," Bob said with a grin. "I want to go for a walk on the beach before our dinner reservations."

"But, Bob"—I looked down at my feet—"I'm wearing pantyhose and high heels."

"Don't worry about it. We'll replace the pantyhose if they get ruined."

The limo drove down Pacific Coast Highway to Balboa Island. Early in our courtship, we'd spent time riding the Ferris wheel, rollerblading, and visiting the restaurants and bars at Balboa Island. It is where we fell in love.

Begrudgingly, I agreed to take a walk on the beach.

Suddenly, I saw a table set for two in a secluded area near the water. It was set with a white tablecloth, formal china, and candles. I did not see anyone around and still hadn't realized this setup was for me.

Bob suggested we sit down at the table. Two men appeared out of nowhere, dressed in full tuxedos, carrying picnic baskets. They brought us appetizers and drinks, then disappeared. They must have watched us from afar and knew precisely when to serve the next course.

I finally realized something special was happening.

Bob had thought of every detail—even a blanket, since he knew I was always cold on the beach.

While the sun set between dinner and dessert, Bob proposed. He promised many romantic nights and a lifetime of adventure together. When we returned to the limo, Bob nodded to the driver. She popped the trunk and released a bunch of helium balloons into the air, then looked at me and said, "They don't make them like this anymore."

Before heading home, we called my dad.

"Dad?" I said when he answered. "Are you asleep? Well, get up and get dressed because Bob and I are on our way to your house."

When we got there, we shared the news about our engagement, then took my dad cruising in the limo to celebrate. It was a special night and time with my father.

I would not have met Bob if my dad hadn't arrived late for our dinner date eight months earlier. Or if he hadn't nagged me endlessly to make the phone call that changed my life.

Besides, my dad and his third wife had been making plans to move out of the country. In a few months, they would move to Fiji, and soon after that to Grenada to own and operate a scuba diving business. This news felt like being abandoned all over again.

By now, I had realized that my dad was incapable of reciprocity. As long as I agreed with all of his viewpoints and was subservient to him, things went smoothly. Otherwise, look out! Reflecting on this experience, I learned that if I'm continuously looking for water in a well I know is dry, I will stay parched. I've also learned there is a lot of gray area in any relationship. It's not all good or all bad. Not all right or wrong. Today I choose to remember the shared experiences we had that warmed my heart and brought me joy at that time in my life.

Now that Bob and I were officially engaged, we picked out a one-carat princess cut diamond, then celebrated over lunch. While I was giddy with excitement, Bob's face looked white and drained; he had spent his entire savings! We both laughed about it, and I knew it indicated his love and commitment to me.

Pre-marriage classes confirmed that we shared the same values around children, money, fidelity, communication, and commitment. But no relationship is stress-free, and shortly before our wedding we found ourselves experiencing some conflict. We reached out to a random Catholic church and asked to meet with a priest.

The priest was smoking a cigarette outside when we met. He had a raspy voice and a good sense of humor. He assured us that everything would be okay and saw it as a strength that we were aware of our conflicts. More importantly, we were willing to work through them.

"What do you need to feel confident moving forward?" he asked in his gravelly voice.

We weren't sure.

"Prayer can help. There is a counsel of older women who run a prayer group. They would consider it a privilege to pray for your marriage. I will ask them to pray for your ceremony and union to have many blessings."

We nodded, moved.

He winked. "Be on the lookout. God will give you a clear sign."

We thanked him for the reassurance, prayer, and promised sign.

Karen and Bob's mother planned a small, intimate wedding for us. On the morning of our wedding day, Bob and I met in Pompano Beach to go for a run. Then we went for a drive in Pat's red Ford Mustang convertible and enjoyed the morning sunshine.

Suddenly, it began to rain. A beautiful rainbow appeared in the sky, and we knew we had received our sign.

I loved teaching, yet found myself feeling limited in the classroom. The students' challenges were rooted in their family of origin. I felt a calling to make a difference in family systems. I quit my job and entered a master's degree program at Chapman University in Orange, California. I substitute taught and waitressed while attending school.

About the same time, Bob grew tired of the late nights and respon-sibilities that go with managing a restaurant chain. He decided to get into the securities industry and become a financial planner.

We were on exciting new paths. Bob was working for a large warehouse in Newport Beach, California. Financial sales was a highly competitive industry, and few trainees made it through to receive their licenses. Bob and I are both Type A personalities; we study hard and perform well.

Chapman University has a community-based center on campus where masters' students like me receive training. Some of the therapy rooms had two-way mirrors. The sessions were taped and reviewed by my supervisors and peers. The clinic had a variety of patients, from chil-dren to adults. We were exposed to a wide variety of diagnoses with the hopes of choosing our specialty areas.

It was excellent training, and even though the feedback we got from supervisors was brutal, it was appreciated. During my training, I learned about the concepts of transference and countertransference. Transference is when the patient unconsciously redirects their feelings onto the therapist. Countertransference is when the therapist directs their feelings onto the patient. I began to have dreams, nightmares, and bizarre reactions from sessions.

The master's degree program required that students participate in five to ten individual therapy sessions.

Despite thinking, *Oh boy, here we go*, I welcomed this and was grateful for the mentors who supported and nurtured my growth. I was encouraged to discuss with my supervisor past traumas that were trig-gered during sessions with patients.

I learned to put a voice to the abuse I suffered and witnessed as a kid. In the classroom, I acquired knowledge about the cycle of domestic violence. I understood why my mother stayed with her abuser for seventeen years. I saw how my father's constant belittling, physical abuse, unpredictability, and financial blackmail methodically brainwashed my mom into thinking she was not a worthy human being. I observed how he apologized after he beat her. He showed remorse, brought her flowers, and committed to never hurt her again. They were all broken promises. The constant criticism stripped her confidence. She began to doubt her opinions and thoughts. Over time, she lost any sense of value in herself. Fortunately, I witnessed my mother break this cycle and rise out of the ashes. She is my hero, and I admire her immensely.

I didn't know what PTSD was at the time. I was relieved to learn about the body's physiological response of fight-flight-freeze, which is designed to protect us from threat or danger. I began to identify the sense of unease I had so often. It also helped me understand why I frequently had the feeling of impending doom. Why I always felt on edge, waiting for the next shoe to drop. Anytime I watched a movie where a man was abusing a woman, I had nightmares and flashbacks of violent events from childhood. The antidote is to stop watching violent movies, which I did. These flashbacks would occur for many years.

I learned a great deal during my training and education at Chapman University. I graduated Cum Laude and was proud of my accomplishments. I learned that it's vital for me, as a therapist, to seek continuous support and guidance when needed.

That said, while I was learning about addiction and abuse, I was drinking. My success and high performance became the basis for my denial. I graduated in 1990 with a master's degree, and then became a licensed marriage and family therapist (LMFT) in 1996. It took six years post master's degree to complete three thousand hours of sessions with clients under a licensed therapist's supervision. I passed the state's written and oral examinations, which required months of rigorous preparation and studying.

I gravitated toward working with adolescents and families. I was fortunate to find a paid internship that turned into a full-time job. I ran an intensive outpatient program (IOP) for adolescents called Back on Track. These teens came to our office from 1:00 p.m. to 5:00 p.m. for group and individual therapy, tutoring, and life skills development. The clinical team required all parents to participate in skills development classes. The philosophy behind Back on Track was to increase services for patients who needed more than outpatient therapy but not the level of hospitalization. Managed care companies liked offering IOP services to their members because it was cost-effective for them.

The founder was a gifted psychologist who was masterful with helping teens and families. He was trained in Eriksonian theory and the king of one-liners. (Erikson was a psychologist and psychoanalyst who developed the eight stages of psychosocial development that helped clinicians to assess and identify age-appropriate functioning.) He was able to bring humor to any situation, so the teens and parents loved him. I did too. He became a mentor, surrogate father, and someone I admired greatly.

I loved working with teenagers. I saw a lot of progress in a short period of time. They made it clear what was on their minds.

My professional life was going well. Southern California was a beautiful place, and we often spent time at the beach. Bob and I had great times drinking with other couples and friends. When I drank too much, I became loud and obnoxious. But it was under the guise of having fun. The dark truth was that it wasn't fun. When I drank, I was hurtful and verbally abusive to Bob at home. When I drank in public, sometimes I embarrassed him.

When my car was rear ended, I was in a neck brace for weeks. I began drinking at night and noticed it relieved my physical pain. My drinking was no longer reserved for weekend parties. Soon I began drinking every day. As my drinking caused conflict in our marriage, Bob and I reached out to the church we attended. It was a nondenominational church, and the pastor was extremely talented. He had previously pastored a megachurch, then stepped down after allegations of impropriety. Frankly, his checkered past made me like him more.

When we started attending his church, Bob and I formed our own opinion regarding his character. Having a public forum can leave people open to scrutiny—and sometimes the allegations hold no credence. This, we discerned, had been the case for Pastor Tim Timmons. He had talent for bringing people to God. When he gave a sermon, I felt like he was speaking directly to me.

Tim had also written a book called *Anyone Anonymous*, which applied the twelve-step recovery program to daily living. I thought he was the perfect person to talk to about my drinking problem.

When I met with him, he began right away with a question. "What does your husband think about your drinking?"

Initially, I thought this was somewhat sexist, but I now realize he knew that family members are often the first to recognize and identify the problem.

This meeting began a beautiful friendship with Tim, his girlfriend (now wife), and the congregation. Bob and I joined Bible studies with other couples and got involved in the church.

Ironically, we socialized and drank with this group of people for several years. My first meeting with him was significant because it was the first time I sought guidance regarding my drinking problem. But I was still having fun and wasn't ready to change.

Tim recognized this and loved me anyway. What I was not able to get from my father was given to me by role models like Tim. He showed unconditional love and regard for me no matter what occurred.

He brought Bob and me to a closer relationship with God, and we are eternally grateful. This felt like a divine intervention and in hindsight, I can see that God always had my back.

My daily drinking continued and progressed. Besides conflict in my marriage, I had no significant consequences. Except, of course, for the internal conflict I experienced daily.

I counseled kids to stay away from drugs and alcohol while I abused alcohol myself.

I was a hypocrite.

I had gone to my first twelve-step meeting in 1996, but I couldn't relate to the people "in the rooms." I had found every reason to magnify our differences and deny I was like them. My life, I had told myself, was nowhere near as screwed up as their lives seemed. The meetings had not been helpful to me, and I didn't relate to their stories. I'd collected many thirty-day chips but had never made the commitment to remain sober.

Bob and I lived in Southern California for nine years in the same two-bedroom apartment. We lived beyond our means and were in debt. We loved Southern California but decided to move to Colorado. Bob knew the area well because he went to undergraduate school at the University of Denver. I was ready for a change after the Northridge Earthquake, Rodney King riots, O. J. Simpson trial, natural disasters, and overall growth of the area.

During the Rodney King riots, I had been working with a group of teens at Back on Track. There had been looting and rioting in the mall next door, as well as a couple of shootings. I had been told to keep the kids safe and waited to release them to their parents. I was so scared, I broke out in hives on my chest, face, and torso.

We had enough of the fast-paced, competitive, and flashy environment of Southern California.

It was time for a new beginning.

KAREN SPEAKS

I loved visiting Kelly and Bob in California. Throughout the years, we explored the state and chalked up numerous adventurous. We hiked near the redwood trees in Northern California, explored the mountains in Big Bear, and rollerbladed at the beaches. A favorite memory was our sunset cruise in Santa Barbara. We had sister trips to Palm Springs and enjoyed our young lives.

Kelly and Bob were generous with their time and spirits. It was magical. We partied hard, but I chalked it up to good, clean fun.

I knew I had a drinking problem but didn't recognize it in Kelly.

Karen goes off to Florida, 19

Karen, 21

Bob and Kelly's wedding,
August 25, 1990

What a family this
Will be!

Mom and Jerry's Wedding, July 6, 1985

10

Kelly's Career Highs

KELLY SPEAKS

It was a culture shock to move from the hustle and bustle of Southern California to Denver, Colorado. We went from six lane highways to two-lane roads. The cashiers at the grocery store might ask how your dog or children were doing.

Frankly, it was irritating at first. Didn't they see the line was three customers deep? Eventually, I realized I was the one with the problem. It was hard to adjust to Colorado's slower pace. I adapted and began to appreciate the beautiful mountain views, generally welcoming people, and a quieter lifestyle. I missed the ocean and beauty of California but enjoyed learning new hobbies like skiing, hiking, and tennis.

Bob launched his own business, Ryan Financial Inc., and built a successful wealth management firm. We purchased our first home and got out of debt. We made new friends, and life was good.

I became the executive director of a twenty-bed group home for adjudicated boys ages thirteen to twenty. Adjudication means these boys were labeled juvenile delinquents, convicted of crimes, and were on probation. The group home was one step closer to them completing their sentence in a normalized environment, while still under supervision and strict guidelines. I was thirty-four years old and was responsible for hiring, training, firing, safety, and overall operations. It was a huge responsibility and memorable learning experience.

The group home was housed in a historical brick building with white pillars constructed in the late 1800s. The three-story house had a spiral staircase—and a history of being haunted! The kids liked this rumor and would share stories of their ghost sightings.

The company's philosophy included activities like white water rafting and hiking for inner-city kids. These new experiences built confidence and provided a way to build self-esteem.

Even though I was the executive director, I had many limitations, the biggest being the budget and salary constraints. Managing the staff was harder than the kids. Particularly the overnight shift. This was a position that required the staff to be awake all night. Their main responsibility was regular bed checks to assure the kids were sleeping soundly. Any new hire required fingerprinting and background checks, so employees were fully vetted. The kids never snitched on the staff or each other, but I would hear conversations and learn things by daily interactions with them.

During one breakfast conversation with the kids, I found out the overnight staff snored loudly. Remember, this was a "wake night" position. The kids said the whole third floor vibrated and joked about how the noise kept them awake.

Another time, I got a call from an angry girlfriend of a different overnight staff. She reported that he brought in alcohol, marijuana, and girls in the middle of the night and partied with the kids. Yikes! After full investigations, they were both terminated.

Most of the staff I hired were young, impressionable, and their hearts were in the right place. I had close relationships with the clinical director and assistant director, who was an ex-college football player from Tennessee. He was buff, athletic, humorous, and he had a great rapport with the kids. He had that wonderful Southern dialect and politeness. We went to happy hours and partied together. Drinking was a way to connect and let off steam. We would come to work hungover the next day and do it all again.

I had been on call twenty-four seven for three years at this point.

I was paged in the middle of the night if a kid didn't come home from pass. I'd be paged if a kid came back loaded from pass. I'd be paged if a staff didn't show up for work. I'd be paged if a kid was threatening or violent toward a staff or student.

The straw that broke the camel's back was when one of the students told me to be careful turning on my car that night. It was a blatant threat, and he had the contacts to harm me. He was back in jail that night, which meant the community was safer.

I was burned out and I was done. I was discouraged by the recidivism, poor outcomes, and lack of resources provided by the state. It was close to impossible to help these kids see there could be another way. I felt defeated.

Alcohol subtly worked its way into my daily routine. Alcoholism snuck up on me, and I do not recall the time or place that I crossed the line. I just know I did. I still didn't see myself as an alcoholic. I had gained twenty pounds and was drinking a lot to cope with the stress of it all.

I quit my job, unsure what I wanted to do next professionally. I was offered a marketing and sales position for a company that provided out-of-home placement for adolescents. I knew nothing about sales and marketing but thought, *Why not?*

The firm wanted to hire a clinician who represented the continuum of services available to families. The corporation became the largest national provider for residential treatment centers across the country. It was a prosperous time for them and me. I had a thirteen-year career with the company, holding various titles and responsibilities.

I was responsible for doing outreach to potential referral sources. These professionals were psychiatrists, licensed therapists, school counselors, educational consultants, hospital facilities, and other professionals specializing in adolescent and young adult interventions. To learn each program's specialty areas, I spent time on the campuses, met the staff, and experienced the unique program components. This training allowed me to go into the community and represent the facilities. I was the liaison between referral sources and the program admissions directors.

I gained a national reputation for my knowledge, integrity, and outreach. I felt that I was making differences and meaningful contributions to families, just not face-to-face in the trenches. I had four different bosses my first five years on the job. Being the first person hired to this department, I felt I was continuously training my superiors.

The fifth boss hit the bulls-eye. She was energetic, disciplined, bright, and a visionary. She built a team that felt like a family. I worked hard to gain her respect and to please her. She knew when to encourage me, support me, and hold me accountable. She was an excellent judge of character and held everyone to a high standard of performance. I learned a great deal from her. We would form a personal friendship that is active today.

I was responsible for coordinating special events, conferences, and program tours. The program tours were experiential. We took part in live cattle drives, rock climbing excursions, and equine therapy activities, to name a few.

These tours involved an endless supply of alcohol. Of course, we didn't serve alcohol around the students, but we took the referral sources out to entertain them. When we toured wilderness programs, we set up elaborate camps and prepared a Dutch oven cookout, serving steaks, baked potatoes, and delicious homemade breads. As part of the evening entertainment, we read cowboy poetry and formed drum circles! We spared no expense, and no detail was overlooked.

Traveling was a large part of my job requirement. I had a national territory and was away from home over 50 percent of the time. It was acceptable to drink on the job, and I had an expense account to wine and dine professionals! How lucky was I?

In addition to territory management, each year I attended multiple industry conferences. I called them "drunk fests." It seemed like a time that everyone let loose. I partook in all of it. Most of the time, I was able to manage my drinking, but there were times that I was sloppy.

One of my most embarrassing incidents was at a conference. After a long day of travel in airports, planes, and rental cars, I checked into the conference hotel. No sooner had I checked in, I was greeted by a top referral source and other professionals who suggested we have a drink.

Several hours of drinking ensued until the bar closed for the night. I had not eaten, and the alcohol went right to my head. I was very drunk, and a good friend who worked for a competing program suggested we order some food and go up to her room. I agreed.

I staggered to the elevator with my friend and the top referral source. While saying good night and laughing in the elevator, I wet my pants. Once in my friend's room, I used the bathroom and hit my head on the counter as I fell off the toilet seat. She was kind, fed me, and made sure that I got to my room safely.

In other circumstances, friends and colleagues saw me drunk but wrote it off as isolated incidents. When I got sober and went public about being an alcoholic, some people said I hid my drinking problem well. Others said it was no surprise. Frankly, my ego told me going public about being an alcoholic was a *really* big deal. Most people didn't care one way or the other. Of course, close friends and colleagues wanted me to be happy and healthy.

Here's what is so perplexing. I was pleased with my career. I took a lot of pride in helping families and professionals find the right services for their children and clients. I knew it was the first step to safety, wellness, and family restoration. I valued the relationships I had with the admissions directors, clinical directors, and executive directors at each program. I admired them greatly and knew the children would be well served at any of the programs.

So, why was I drinking alone in hotel rooms?

Why was I causing conflict in my marriage?

Why didn't I answer my phone at night?

Did I have a problem?

There were moments of clarity. I recognized that even though I had a great job, husband, and financial success, I abused alcohol. I was like a sleek vehicle, shiny on the outside but rusted on the inside. Just don't look under the hood.

After the fleeting moments of clarity passed, I would justify my behavior and point the finger at someone else who *clearly* had a problem. This became my go-to pattern of denial.

And I could always compare myself with Karen. Obviously, *she* was the one with a problem. She had multiple arrests, car accidents, and alcohol had ruined her life. I continued establishing relationships with people who liked to party as much or more than I did.

On the other hand, entertaining was part of my job description. I did more than just "hold down" a job. I was one of the highest performers on the team. I never had any legal trouble. I never missed a mortgage payment. I had a great husband.

I had yet to learn that rock bottom doesn't look the same for all of us. But it's still rock bottom.

Fortunately, there were people on the team who were in recovery. Also, I had friends who lived happy, sober lives. Sometimes, when I had a moment of clarity and could admit I was in crisis, I reached out to one of them. One lady in particular, Lola, took me to a woman's twelve-step meeting and supported me. She also talked to me about the concept of "yet." *Yet* is a compelling word. She would remind me that I hadn't been fired . . . yet.

I hadn't gotten a divorce or a DUI . . . yet.

Whenever Lola noticed me drinking again, she never chastised or judged me. She simply said she guessed I wasn't done drinking yet. She left the door open for when I was ready to accept help.

I had many resources, and when I was ready for help, I knew where to go. At the same time, I was a daily drinker and had no idea how to stop. All previous attempts had failed.

KAREN SPEAKS

Kelly did a good job of hiding her drinking and keeping her secret. She was living my dream life. Her job looked glamorous to me. I admired her professional and financial success as well as the exciting places she traveled. Who gets to play at a dude ranch and call it a job?

How could she possibly be an alcoholic?

11

Kelly Gets Sober

KELLY SPEAKS

I got sober on July 13, 2005.

As I write this, I am sixteen years sober. Getting sober was one of the most challenging tasks I have experienced in my life. The idea of never having another drink was overwhelming and, frankly, depressing. How was I expected to not enjoy a drink at a celebration like a wedding, graduation, birthday, anniversary, holiday, or any special occasion? How was I to cope while attending a funeral? I drank daily, so how was I going to learn to live without alcohol?

This sounds dramatic, but there are many paradoxes in recovery. I remember feeling like my life was over. I wanted to stop drinking but living without using alcohol as a daily crutch was unknown territory for me. I thought I'd never have fun again. On the outside, I had a great job, husband, home, and appeared very successful. But on the inside, I felt desperate, alone, and lost. I dedicated my life to helping others. I was an "expert" on intervention and adolescent development. I was living a lie and my life was certainly not in alignment with my values.

For the first time in my life, I was willing to admit complete defeat from alcohol. As much as I wanted to say it was fun, somewhere along the line, it was controlling me, not the other way around.

This time felt different than the many other times I said I was going to quit.

This time I was willing to do what was suggested.

This time I was desperate enough to listen to others who had success staying sober. This time I'd look for the similarities with people's life experiences instead of the differences.

This time I'd admit I knew nothing.

KAREN SPEAKS

Kelly is an educated, poised, and beautiful woman. She was not in the habit of airing her dirty laundry. We were visiting Mom when she spilled her guts and said her husband was leaving her because of her drinking.

I was shocked. Even though she had never been in any legal or financial trouble, her brokenness and confusion were the same as every real alcoholic.

In our recoveries, I noticed that it has been total strangers who have been able to help us. I'm not sure why that is. Our family's greatest desire was to help. *The only thing I can attribute this to is that strangers have no emotional investment in you. If you don't succeed, it doesn't matter to them; therefore you can't hurt them or disappoint them.*

KELLY SPEAKS

Here's the formula that worked for me: I attended ninety meetings in ninety days. I got a sponsor and did the steps. I didn't drink no matter what. I took one day at a time. Sometimes it was necessary for me to take one minute or one hour at a time.

The one day at a time concept was powerful for me. I believed the reason I continued to relapse previously was I'd get overwhelmed by the idea I could *never* have another drink. I would say "fuck it" and sabotage myself. One day at a time seemed manageable. I wanted to be happy, joyous, and free, which is one of the many promises of sobriety.

I attended women's meetings. I felt at home there and felt unconditional acceptance and love. The ladies didn't judge, and they allowed me to move at my pace. During the first eighteen months, I sat in the back of the room in the corner, held a box of tissues, cried, and listened intently to others.

When I finally shared, the women came up to me, thanked me, and said they enjoyed getting to know me. There is something beautiful about people who attend meetings, whose sole purpose is to help another alcoholic who is struggling. Of course, I'd ask myself, *What do they want from me? Why are they so nice? What's in it for them?*

I didn't think I would respond well to behavior modification, but I sure looked forward to getting my chips! Most meetings give chips and recognize thirty, sixty, and ninety days of sobriety, then begin to give six-month, nine-month, and one-year chips. I found meetings that recognized every month! I loved the recognition, clapping, and acknowledgment of my hard work. I was proud of every small step and another day sober. The chips mean the world to me, and I pass them on to newcomers today.

My husband attended many AA meetings with me, but when he saw me get my one-year chip, it meant the world to me! My mom and stepdad told me all the time how proud of me they were.

I'm not sure that any average drinker can understand alcoholism or addiction, but my family consistently acknowledges my sobriety. Each year for my sobriety anniversary, my mom and stepdad send me an engraved charm with a word or phrase, such as "gratitude" or "you are a miracle" or "strength," reflecting the year of my sobriety. Thus far, I have sixteen charms! This beautiful gesture of love makes me smile and cry at the same time.

I was broken and disgusted with myself, so I didn't need a confrontational sponsor. I was my own worst critic and could beat myself up better than anyone else could. I needed someone who would be direct with me, but also nurturing. I'm so grateful to my sponsors, who were willing to be patient, give their time freely, and support me through the steps! They have become trusted friends. I began to seek guidance and take the suggestions of successful people living a sober lifestyle.

My first big challenge was attending the wedding of my youngest sister, Kolleen. My sponsor suggested that I not attend, but I couldn't fathom not being at my little sis's wedding. I was six weeks sober and knew the reception would be an open bar. I knew my father was attending, which always threw the family into an emotional tailspin. I knew there would be challenges with Karen because we never knew what drugs she was using. I knew there would be tension between my stepdad and Dad—so much unpredictability.

Karen was "sober," meaning that she wasn't drinking. However, to our surprise, Karen and Kendra got drunk on the plane to California. Once they landed, the lies, drama, and chaos ensued. She skillfully found a reason to go into the apartment of a relative and beeline it to his bathroom. We thought this was odd behavior and later realized she stole his pain pills from his medicine cabinet. She also ruffled through all the cosmetic bags, purses, and personal items of family members. She stole muscle relaxers, anxiety pills, and other prescribed medications. There was no shortage of drama.

My father invited me out to the pool to visit. He was drinking a pitcher of beer at ten in the morning. He said, "Pull up a chair and have a drink." He knew I had not had a drink in six weeks and was trying to stay sober. This invitation hurt me. I believe this was not purposefully malicious behavior. I think other people have no idea how hard it is for someone newly sober to be around alcohol.

Guests enjoyed expensive liquor flowing freely at the open bar. All the liquor was top-shelf. I didn't drink hard liquor—I was a wino—but my mouth salivated anyway. I don't remember much about the ceremony or reception. Anxiety paralyzed me. I relied on Bob for support.

I listened to the guidance I had gotten before the wedding. I had my own rental car. I stayed at a hotel, not Kolleen's house. I had my sponsor on speed dial. I prayed for sanity in the bathroom stall. I had an escape plan. I was fortunate to have a husband who supported me in getting sober and wanted to do anything to help me stay that way. This was my first sober wedding. The "firsts" are always tough: first holiday, first funeral, first birthday. Somehow, getting through one day at a time accumulates to weeks, months, and years.

I could begin to see that there was a different way.

Enclosed is a poem I wrote in my fifth year of sobriety, dedicated to the women in my home group meeting.

May 31, 2010
I walked into the room, trembling, alone, and so scared.
Frightened to ask for help
Humiliated that I needed it

Ashamed to be there

Desperate for a solution.

The room was so loud with laughter, chatter, and hugs.

I was overwhelmed. The noise was startling.

There were so many women smiling!

Introductions: Oh No

My name is Kelly, and I'm an al-co-hol-ic.

Panic ran through my body, and with this admission came tears.

Tears of shame,

Tears of humiliation,

Tears of confusion,

Tears of hope.

I thought that maybe, just maybe, if it worked for all of these women, it could work for me too.

A room of total strangers embraced me, loved me, and offered me unconditional acceptance.

For this, I'm eternally grateful.

Kelly R.

12

Another Geographical Cure

KAREN SPEAKS

Ready for a fresh start, my boyfriend and I enjoyed our vacation in the little town of Deland, Florida (Mayberry RFD, right?). In fact, we found the perfect house: a yellow charmer that evoked images of white picket fences, little kids playing in the front yard, and being active in the community.

Yellow homes seemed like happy places to me, so I figured this was a good omen. The rural area reminded me of my childhood roots, and the view from my front window framed cows and horses running in the field. Plus, my adorable yellow home was on a dead-end street, which is where I was headed anyway.

It was perfect. I was thrilled to escape my life in South Florida. I just wanted to be someone else, anyone other than me. And I was certain this was the place where that could happen.

In recovery circles, an alcoholic's belief that moving to a new area will leave problems behind and create a fresh start is commonly known as a "geographic cure." What we don't realize is that, when we move, we take ourselves along.

I didn't yet understand that wherever I lived, the common denominator was always me.

We lived a frugal lifestyle and had a hefty savings account. The only thing we wasted money on was drugs and the legal issues related to them. That added up quickly.

I worked for a few months at a small timeshare company at a resort in Palm Coast, Florida—just long enough to meet a few kindred spirits living the party lifestyle.

It did not take me long to get right back on the merry-go-round. I found new connections to buy drugs and got to work creating the same life I left.

I got deeply involved in the pill mill clinics. It was a real racket. The office locations were sketchy, and the rent was cheap. The business hours were random, operating three to four hours per day with pharmacies on site. All I had to do was show up with plenty of cash, an X-Ray, or an MRI to get the drugs I needed.

Given my entrepreneurial spirit, I soon figured out how to supply my addiction and make extra money on the side. I recruited other addicts and drove a caravan around to the pill mills to collect prescriptions. I got them filled then doled out the agreed number of pills to my team of addicts for their services—after taking my cut, of course. A typical visit cost between $200 to $250 for the scripts plus the inflated price of drugs. The controlled substances could cost thousands of dollars per visit. I got burned often. Fool me once, shame on you; fool me twice, shame on me. I learned to activate the child locks in the car after someone bolted with my money and goods. I was living in a disgusting, sleazy world.

As the practice became commonplace, pharmacies couldn't keep up with the demand for the inventory. It took weeks before they could fill the scripts. In the meantime, everyone was trying to stay high.

The crowd I knew and hung around with became more dangerous. It was not unusual to be traveling with guns and robbing each other. I glamorized this lifestyle. I thought it was cool. My cell phone rang off the hook—all day, all night—with people wanting to buy drugs.

I visited walk-in clinics with made-up injuries claiming excruciating pain. Before the powers that be caught on, it was easy to do. Eventually, the walk-in clinics started to get hip to my game. I was escorted out of a few offices and notified by letter not to return due to "pill seeking behavior."

I laughed so hard when I received that first letter, chalking it up to doctors playing the "cover your ass" game. I did not see the severity of my situation. I justified my actions with statements like, "I pay my bills, and I'm independent, so I can do what I want. I am a full-grown adult. I don't owe anybody any explanations."

Of course, that was my arrogance talking. To me, if I paid my bills, that equaled a manageable lifestyle. I never believed my life was unmanageable.

My resistance to the truth almost killed me several times. I see that as false pride. I never admitted I did not know how to do something, even when it was blatantly obvious.

Then there was the self-pity. I secretly denied feeling sorry for myself. I knew real grown-ups did not walk around with a chip on their shoulder, thinking the world owed them something because they did not have a picture-perfect start.

I was emotionally stunted, pretending to be the person I presented to the world. I wore a mask and was able to adapt to any situation.

But my facade became harder and harder to keep up as time went on, and I sunk lower and lower.

One weekend, my mother, sisters, and I were in San Antonio, Texas, for a vacation. My phone rang three times in fifteen minutes.

My sister Kendra looked at me. "Karen," she said, "I cannot believe you have sunk low enough to be a drug dealer."

I was shocked and insulted. I denied her accusation vehemently, but she knew the truth. And she was right. I felt so dirty. This was not how I was raised. I knew right from wrong. I had become not only addicted to drugs but enmeshed in the lifestyle.

One day I drove about thirty miles to a walk-in clinic for some pills. The doctor would not give me a narcotic; instead, he prescribed Indocin, a potent anti-inflammatory drug. I knew that this was a waste of my time as that drug wouldn't get me high. Then I noticed the script was just a letter or two different from a common narcotic named Endocet. I decided to take the prescription home and change it a tiny bit. It also reflected zero refills, so what would be the harm in adding "one refill" to the label? I fancied myself an amateur pharmacist.

I took it to my local Walmart pharmacy to get filled. I told my boyfriend I would call him when I was leaving the store, pills in hand. I dropped off the script and did a little shopping. An hour later my prescription wasn't ready yet, so I ran my groceries home and came back.

As I approached the pharmacy counter, my intuition screamed at me to leave the prescription there and turn around. But my craving overpowered all rational thought.

I thought I was home free when the pharmacist handed me the bag. I was almost to the exit when the stores' rent-a-cop grabbed my elbow and steered me to their hidden interrogation room. The local police were waiting there for me.

I played dumb as a rock, but it did no good. I was arrested for prescription fraud. I tried to get them to give my boyfriend the pills because I had paid for them. After all, if they weren't going to give me a refund, I should be able to keep them, right?

My thinking was becoming more irrational, devious, and criminal.

I retained an attorney. She was able to get the felony charge reduced, and I was put on probation for six months. As part of probation, I was mandated to attend twelve-step meetings, participate in individual and group drug counseling, and complete community service hours. I also had to give random urine analysis (UAs). But I managed to find creative ways to acquire clean urine.

None of this bothered me. I went through the motions and did what was required. At this point, I knew way more about addiction and drug use than any counselor unless they were also an addict. I could never let myself accept their help or suggestions. I secretly thought they were stupid and out of their depth with tricky, crafty me. There goes that ego coming through again.

The absolute worst punishment was when Walmart put my picture on what I called the wall of shame. The wall included pictures of shoplifters and other people banned from the store due to criminal behavior. Banned from my local Walmart? No way. These people were ruining my life.

I shopped at Walmart almost every day. In fact, part of the reason I bought the yellow house was that it was only half a mile from Walmart's front door.

This wouldn't do at all. I decided I could not live banned from Walmart, so I donned a pair of sunglasses and a baseball hat and walked right in, my head held high. No one kicked me out. Apparently, they had forgotten all about me, and I could go about my shopping in peace.

What a relief!

Despite my arrest, nothing had really changed at all.

13

Codependency Sucks

KAREN SPEAKS

Nanny Burd still lived in South Florida. She was alone, in her mid-eighties, with no family nearby to help her. Before moving to Deland, I had been her only emotional support. She was not one to make friends easily, so I was it. I handled all her business affairs, paid bills, sold property, etc. I was trustworthy and competent with her finances.

Now that I was in Deland, I desperately wanted her to live with me. There was plenty of room at my house and no reason for her to live alone, despite the fact that she was a proud, stubborn woman who insisted she was okay.

One day we got news that lit her world up and got her packing her bags. My father, who had been living outside of the country on the island of Grenada for some time, was moving to Deland and bringing his Grenada family with him.

Unlike Nanny Burd, I was less than thrilled. In fact, I was scared to death. His presence was too big for me to deal with. I wasn't afraid of the violence anymore—I was smart enough to leave—but the unpredictability, emotional abuse, and verbal abuse that came with him overwhelmed me.

Plus, I knew that he was beating his current wife and children. I knew this because his wife had told me. I couldn't save them, and it was too painful being around them knowing my dad was doing to them what he had done to us.

But, being a good little people pleaser, I went into full superhero mode. I thought I knew what was best for everyone. When they arrived, I found my dad a home, arranged a mortgage, and did all the general grunt work. All the while, he drank. He got a job selling real estate and made me his unpaid personal assistant.

I have to admit, he excelled in his new career. My father was not just a drunk. He had many talents. Sales was one of them. That was something I admired and respected about my father. When he set his mind to something, it happened.

Somehow, by sheer will alone, he had started and sold successful businesses, traveled the world, and was a good friend to many people. But his refusal to quit drinking made him a real Dr. Jekyll and Mr. Hyde at home. Add alcohol, shake, stir, and the dark side emerged.

The funny thing was, I understood this because I was the same way. The only thing I saw my dad fail at was his close personal relationships and his ability to put down the booze. When the monster appeared, people got scared.

Nanny Burd, excited about her son's move to Deland, couldn't move fast enough to join him. Sometimes she stayed with my boyfriend and me, sometimes with dad and his family. But before long, she begged me to find her an affordable apartment because she couldn't stand the chaos and drama at either home.

When Dad made some serious financial mistakes and his house went into foreclosure, he borrowed money from my grandmother to move his family back to Grenada.

A lot of money.

Many things transpired during his time here that hurt us deeply. I had hoped our relationship would be different this time and we could have a real connection. I was always hoping. I made excuses for his behavior, but the truth is my well-being was just not that important to him. If I handled his affairs, I was a good and valuable human being. If I didn't, then look out. If I did what everyone wanted me to do, I thought I was worth loving. If I didn't, I was tossed aside as useless. Not until my recovery began did I learn what real unconditional love looks like. Now, I don't believe any human is fully capable of unconditional love—only God can do that—but some people are better at it than others. My dad wasn't even in the ballpark.

Dad and I had an unspoken agreement not to talk about my drug addiction or his drinking. If we didn't acknowledge the issue, then maybe it didn't exist.

Nanny Burd and I had the same unspoken agreement. Over the next few years, as her health declined, I accompanied her to her doctor appointments and acted as her mouthpiece. Every time a doctor asked about her symptoms, she looked at me to tell them. That worked out okay for me because I manipulated the arrangement for drugs. She would get a prescription filled, and I'd steal it. It worked for a long time.

She knew what I was doing, and I knew she knew. She never confronted me. We loved each other very much but had an unhealthy relationship. My drug habit became crazy expensive. It cost a lot of money even with the side hustles. I had an intuitive feeling that something was going to break.

I was driving home after a drug deal on a familiar road I had driven many times. My brain snapped. I just kept driving back and forth on that road. I didn't recognize where I should turn to get home. In my confusion, I stopped driving and called someone to come and help me.

Waiting for help to arrive, I sat in my car and stared at a pile of pills in my hand. I had just purchased about sixty high-powered opiates, and suddenly the thought came to me that I was holding the batch that would kill me. I knew if I took any more of them, I would die.

Sometimes nonsensical words came out of my mouth even when my brain knew they made no sense. We used to laugh and call it scrambled eggs. I nodded out in public frequently. I behaved like a junkie.

But I'd never had *this* feeling before. It was a terrifying premonition.

I gave that handful of pills to the friend who arrived to help me. I told him I did not care what he did with them. He made one thousand dollars on that batch. Boy, was I mad at myself when the withdrawals started!

When I told Kelly what had happened and asked for help, she said she would help me get into a rehab program. She had connections because she was a professional in that field. She set something up per my request, and I then ghosted her. I had a deep distrust for doctors at this point in my life.

Terrified of going into full-blown withdrawals due to my previous experience, I started alternating between using opiates and taking Suboxone, an opiate blocker. If I had paid attention to my body, I would have noticed the deterioration, but I did not. I knew I was skinny and looked older than I was, but I still believed that I could never be too thin or too rich.

I had another awakening experience. Doing some mindless shopping, I went into the dressing room. As I was peeling off my sundress to try on some clothes, I noticed I was urinating on the floor. I could not stop the flow. I hadn't felt it coming on or coming out.

I was utterly shocked. How could that happen? How could I not feel anything?

Grabbing my things, I ran out of the store. On the way, I stopped to tell an employee that someone had an accident in the dressing room. Of course, I was too ashamed to admit it was me.

It was the oddest experience for my body to betray me like that. I'd never been out of control of bodily functions—at least not unless I was blackout drunk. But I wasn't drinking now. I'd had my go-round with alcohol. I considered myself cured of that. Now I was just doing drugs.

I didn't understand that for someone like me, all substances were off the table. I could not ever use any drug or alcohol safely.

People used to joke, "Only quitters go to twelve-step groups." I wanted to be a quitter. In fact, I'd attended some of those meetings but concluded I was different from the others. I thought I was too far gone for help.

Little did I know I was just your everyday garden-variety drunk and addict. I found out later that my inability to be honest with myself at a heart level kept me sick for years. I was too full of shame to share the truth with anyone about who I really was.

I called Kelly and told her about my pee-pee incident. I had no clue how deeply I frightened her. I was consumed with my selfish life and couldn't see the forest through the trees. I promised her for the umpteenth time that I would stop.

I was finally alarmed enough to make an appointment with an addiction specialist. He prescribed more Suboxone, which I took as recommended. I was clean for ten days. This was a triumph because I had not been sober that long in years. To me, that was a big success.

But when I told people I'd been sober for more than a week, no one believed me. I would not have believed me either. I had turned into an awful liar.

My mom used to say that if she asked me something point-blank, I would tell her the truth.

Not anymore. I had changed. My moral barometer was at a five on a scale of 1 to 100.

KELLY SPEAKS

By now, I had been sober for about five years. Words can't describe the level of helplessness, desperation, and fear my family and I felt regarding Karen's drug addiction.

We had endless phone calls and shared many tears, anger, and confusion about why and how someone could slowly but surely be killing themselves.

What were we to do?

What's interesting is that at the same time my family was at a loss as to our next step, I was helping other families take those exact steps and find solutions and hope.

I had gained enough experience and confidence by then to launch my own business called GPS Family Consulting, providing guidance, purpose, and solutions to families.

It had been a huge decision and risk to leave the security of the company I had worked with for thirteen years, where I had a guaranteed salary, benefits, and meaningful friendships. I was grateful for the colleagues I'd had the privilege to work with. Their dedication to children and families would forever be part of their legacy. I credited the training and support I received from my boss and others in instilling the foundation I needed to be successful with new endeavors.

In other words, I'd been prepared well for a new challenge.

Still, I had prayed for clarity and validation that launching my business was the right decision. While taking a walk one day, enjoying nature, I'd clearly heard, "It is time. You are ready."

What? Can You please repeat that?

I don't often hear voices, but when I do, I know they are messages from the divine, so I listen! How exciting for me to get such confirmation.

On another walk, I'd heard, "G.P.S.: guidance, purpose, solutions." Wow!

What great confirmation and validation that I was on the right path. As I launched my company, one of my areas of expertise was working with families who had troubled adolescents or young adults. These challenges included a wide range of diagnoses: mood, personality, and substance abuse disorders, to name a few.

I also worked with learning differences and autism spectrum disorders. Families hired me to work collaboratively with schools, communities, and other professionals to complete objective assessments of their loved ones. The evaluation included recommendations regarding the best program options, level of care, and the child and family's best path. Typically, families had exhausted local resources and, due to safety concerns, needed out-of-home placement. Once placement occurred, I provided case management and liaison services between the residential facility and the family.

Families hired me to assist them through one of the most challenging and turbulent times of their lives. The sense of fear, frustration, and helplessness of these parents was palpable. I was honored when a family engaged my services. I believed my compassion and empathy were evident, as well as my ability to instill hope for positive outcomes. I worked with families whose children had multiple suicide attempts, overdoses, and engaged in self-harming behaviors. These conditions were exasperated by co-occurring disorders. Situations were crisis-driven and required immediate intervention.

Operating my business and supporting families through crisis-driven situations was a huge growth experience. Talk about countertransference! Initially, I was frustrated and confused about why some parents would pay for my services but refuse to accept my guidance. They seemed more interested in maintaining the existing chaos. In contrast, other families were so desperate for a solution, they would do anything suggested to create change in their relationships. Their desperation and openness to guidance mirrored my recovery process.

There is an acronym in AA called HOW It stands for honesty, open-mindedness, and willingness. I realized I had to become honest, open-minded, and willing. I couldn't make any parent do anything they weren't ready to do. I couldn't make them conform to my recommendations. I couldn't make them comply with the placement process. I couldn't make them want to evaluate their part and resolve their traumas. These circumstances allowed me to work on my issues of judgment and control. I learned through time how to guide and coach others. Much like the concepts of the twelve steps, I could make suggestions but had to accept when people chose a different path. Outcomes for families varied based upon the parents' willingness to roll up their sleeves and engage in the therapeutic process. Given these adolescents and young adults had chronic conditions, the outcomes were mediocre even under the best of circumstances.

Families are unique with their strengths, life experiences, and challenges. I understood there was nothing more painful to parents than their child struggling and them not being able to "fix it."

I knew every professional and personal experience I had led me to be uniquely qualified to help guide parents through this journey.

And yet when it came to helping Karen and our family, why did I feel so helpless?

It was time to practice what I'd been preaching.

14

The Dreaded Intervention

KAREN SPEAKS

One bright and sunny morning in August, as I sat on my couch watching TV, four cars pulled into my driveway like the house was on fire.

I stared warily out the window. I didn't recognize the cars. But soon enough I recognized the people inside when the car doors opened, and members of my family climbed out.

Oh no! This was the dreaded intervention!

They had traveled from Texas and Colorado with letters in hand and a fierce determination to help me. This was no joke. They had spent serious money to get this together and pull this off.

They didn't wait for an invitation. Everyone barged in and sat down in the living room.

"I've seen this show on TV," I joked. "So where on the television crews?"

Of course, they'd brought no cameras. But they *had* brought a transport agent to make sure I got into the rehab

facility if I agreed to go. My brain flooded with memories of the
Nut House when I was young. The Goon Squad was hard to
forget. My life must be one bad dream. I did not see the point
in going to treatment. I had two reasons for that: One, I thought
I knew more than anyone else about me. Two, who would be
paying for this? I was not worth that much money. I was certain
I would fail.

Deep down inside, I knew the real reason I was going to
say no was this: I had no faith at all in any program. Actually, I
had no faith at all—in anything. I have heard that faith is hope
with a track record. My track record was one of failure, disas-
ter, and disappointment to anyone who loved me, especially
my family. I felt like they should cut their losses, protect their
hearts, and go home.

They were steadfast in following through with their mission. Poor Kelly had the job of following me around the house
to police me. They brought drugs so I would not withdraw before getting to detox. No one believed that I had not used for
ten days.

I was insulted by that at the time, but now I see it as an
extremely kind gesture.

My first objection was the location: Houston. What? If you
think Florida is hot in the summer, then go to Houston. I knew
their fear was I would not go.

I listened to letters written and read by my mother, stepdad,
sisters, and their spouses. The letters did not feel judgmental.
The letters were a plea for me to stop killing myself. They were
a plea for me to choose life. They reflected the depth of the love
my family had for me. They were a reminder of the real me, the
person I used to be: someone they missed dearly and wanted

back in their lives. The person I might still have a chance to reclaim. The person God created me to be.

I so wanted to be that person for them, but I didn't think it was possible.

I opened my mouth to say *No, I don't want to go.* But then I looked at my mother and saw that her head was bobbing, and her hands were trembling.

And with that glance at her feeble condition, I reluctantly agreed to my family's plan.

Kelly had my suitcase packed so fast my head spun. In practically minutes, we were out the door and on the way to the airport with the escort. I was so angry. I was on my way to treatment in Houston, Texas. Ugh!

KELLY SPEAKS

At the time of Karen's intervention, I had five years of sobriety under my belt. Additionally, because of my profession, I'd had the good fortune of touring national treatment programs and meeting knowledgeable colleagues who provided us with valuable guidance.

My family had lots of questions and looked to me to provide answers.

Is it the right time for an intervention? How does it work? What will it cost? How do we evaluate whether it's successful or not? Who should participate?

My experience helped me realize that Karen's intervention was really for our family. It would be the first clear boundary that we set to change unhealthy patterns of enabling. This was vital if we were to feel that we had left no stone unturned, that we had tried everything possible to offer Karen help.

Our goal was to have a forum to express our profound fears and concerns for her and create a path to sobriety for her—while at the same time letting go of our expectations or attachment to the outcome. Whether she accepted the support or not wasn't the issue. As you can imagine, this makes sense in theory, but is difficult to do in practice.

Our other goal was to allow Mother to have a voice and lead the charge.

A friend of mine named Robert Martinez owned a company called The Gift of Recovery. He generously offered to do Karen's intervention for the cost of his travel and ancillary fees. I arranged a bed for her at an adult recovery center in Houston, Texas.

Our family spent the evening before the intervention reviewing protocol. The interventionist did a great job of preparing us for the possible scenarios of the next day.

While my mother and stepfather were willing to second mortgage their home to pay for treatment for Karen, the interventionist stressed the importance of Karen owning her experience—and part of this meant taking financial responsibility. Karen was forty-nine years old and had her own financial resources. Plus, I had negotiated a discounted rate with the CEO to contain the cost, which would help. This was a great opportunity. I'm sure if you combined her lawyer's fees for previous arrests and the costs of her drug use, she could have paid for treatment three times over.

The interventionist knew about my family history. He had supported my recovery and, over the years, taken my desperate and tearful phone calls regarding Karen. He explained to all of us that, during the intervention, it was vital for me to be a sister and a daughter, *not* a professional or expert. We all agreed that I would only talk when prompted. I was to allow other family members—especially my mom—to take the lead.

This strategy took a lot of pressure off me and successfully changed the dynamics of the situation. My mother, stepfather, and sister had so many beautiful, affirming things to say. It was lovely to be an observer and hear their insights.

I was, however, put in the role of "policing" Karen and followed her around her house. I was told to help her pack a bag, follow her to the restroom, and avoid her popping any pills along the way.

As the intervention unfolded, complicated dynamics with the people in Karen's life began to be revealed. Despite Karen's boyfriend being the person who called us saying Karen needed help, he kept telling her that interventions don't work and pressured her to tell us to leave once we were there doing the intervention. Even knowing she was out of control, he was protecting himself. Plus, if Karen's lifestyle changed, then his would too. He had a lot to lose: He was a chronic relapser. He and Karen partied together. He hadn't been employed during their relationship. He was happy with the routine and didn't want us to rock the boat.

Then there were logistical complications with Nanny. Karen was responsible for taking care of our ninety-three-year-old grandmother, who was in a long-term care facility. When we visited with Nanny and told her Karen needed to go away for a while and get treatment, she was distraught and confused. We took a video of her crying and pleading for Karen to stay in treatment and get the help she needed. We sent it to Karen while she was in flight to the treatment center. It felt like emotional blackmail, but we pulled no punches demonstrating how her drug use affected her loved ones.

Issues with our father were, as you can imagine, complex on many levels. By this time, he had now divorced his fourth wife. He had also pressured Karen into taking care of him—managing everything for him including errands, grocery shopping, and medical issues. And even though we were all adults—and Mom had been remarried for twenty-five years—being around our father could easily trigger the physical and emotional abuse we suffered in our childhood.

We made plans to meet with Dad and tell him what had happened and how long Karen would be gone. There was a lot of drama around contacting and meeting with him. Mom had not seen him in years, and we knew his behavior was unpredictable. And while our stepfather was a blessing in our lives and was fiercely protective, we asked him not to be present when we met with Dad. It added pressure and unneeded stress.

We all felt extremely protective of our mother. Kolleen and I coached Mom and said if Dad got demeaning, aggressive, or abusive in any way, she was to leave the room immediately.

We promised we would not be far behind her. We would simply let him know what had occurred and give him some documents related to the care of Nanny Burd.

We met my father at my grandmother's nursing home. When we told him about Karen's intervention, the first thing out of his mouth was a bitter complaint:

"What am I supposed to do about your grandmother?"

The second thing he had to say was this:

"When will you learn to stop interfering with people's lives?"

I remember feeling sad for Karen. After spending time with the people closest to her, it became clear they had zero care and concern for her welfare. They were all just using her for her money, time, and to meet their own selfish needs. Of course, my grandmother wasn't using Karen in a vindictive way, but she had become utterly dependent upon her and had been for years. Karen's payoff was access to all of Nanny Burd's fentanyl patches and oxycodone pills.

On the day of the intervention, we drove up and surprised Karen at her home. I knew my sister well and suspected that she might agree to the intervention because she wouldn't want to hurt or disappoint our mother. I knew she would want to minimize any pain Mom experienced.

Below is my intervention letter to Karen, as well as my mother's. I hope it is helpful to anyone who may be curious about the process.

Dear Karen:

I have always felt blessed to have you as my older sister. When we were growing up, I thought that we were inseparable. I was complimented when people asked if we were twins because I thought you were so beautiful with that fantastic smile and twinkle in your eyes. We were each other's "rock." No matter what was happening, we knew we could count on each other. I admired how smart you were and how easy school was for you.

I loved your sense of adventure and won't ever forget our bungee jumping experience at Elitches amusement park. Talk about twins; we were bound together so tightly that whatever happened, we were going to experience it together. I loved your desire to want to try new things and remember renting roller blades on the beach, doing aerobics, and other fun things together in Florida.

Karen, as you know, our family has a long history of addicts and alcoholics. We know firsthand how this disease destroys loved ones and hurts family members. When you were arrested for prescription fraud and charged with a felony, I was so afraid that you were going to spend a long time in jail. When you called me after a 24-hour hold in the psychiatric hospital and asked for help, I was so proud of you and knew the courage it took to pick up the phone. When you changed your mind only 24 hours later, I was disappointed and angry. I've grown not to trust you or depend on you in any way because of the continued lies, stealing, and broken promises. I've seen the drugs turn you into someone that I don't recognize.

Karen, you have always had a big heart and often put other people's needs ahead of yourself. I want my sister back. I know the isolation, fear, loneliness, guilt, and shame addiction causes. I know that you have the courage and strength to accept the help that is being offered today. I know that deep down, this is the opportunity you have been waiting for. I know that sometimes God has to do for us what we can't do for ourselves. Will you accept the help that is being offered to you today?

Love, Kelly

Dear Karen,

I am so proud of you and all your success in your life. The love I felt when I first held you in my arms is indescribable. A perfect baby. Even one with dimples. "Isn't She Lovely"? You are just a wonderful gift to me from God. You are such a passionate person with a beautiful sense of humor. You put warmth and feeling in everything you do. You enjoy being with family, especially for holidays, mostly Christmas. I am in amazement watching you opening your gifts—the sparkle in your eyes and the laughter we all share. Remember the trips we took using license plates to play cards and making up words from all the signs we passed? You always won the word games. How about the fair with the miniature horses? You all had a good laugh on me.

Karen, you were always there for me whenever I needed a shoulder. Your strength and advice always made me feel better. Karen, I love you more than life itself. When I don't hear from you for a while, I begin to think that you are using drugs again. I feel frustrated and worried. When Jerry and I came to get you from Pat's house and brought you to Texas for treatment, I could hardly keep my breath; my whole body trembled. I felt scared, helpless, and afraid. A few years ago, your visit to Texas was problematic for the entire month you were here. Although you went to therapy, you still stopped at those care centers to get drugs. You lied to me. I returned to Florida with you because of the situation that was going on there. I'll never forget seeing you unable to talk or stay awake because of the drugs you took. My heart broke to see you that way.

Karen, I can't imagine what life would be like without you. The pain would be unbearable for me. I can't lose the precious gift God has given me. This disease, with the right help, can lead you to recovery. You have so much to offer, and no one can recover alone. Look how many times you have tried before. Karen, reach out to others. I want you to be free to be the person you were meant to be. I love you with all my heart. Reclaim your life as the loving, caring daughter you are. Don't waste the wonderful life you have been given. Will you please accept the help we are offering today?

Your loving mother

Was the intervention successful? I guess this depends on how you define success. I believe it was because we planted a seed. We created a moment of clarity and interrupted a pattern for Karen. We were given the gift of professional guidance that provided a safe environment to share our love and desires for Karen. We had taken action in a situation that seemed hopeless. We could rest knowing that we did our best to provide Karen with a path to sobriety, health, and wellness.

But as the saying goes: "You can lead a horse to water, but you can't make him drink."

KAREN SPEAKS

I don't remember who drove to the airport, but my escort, Robert, made sure I got to Houston uneventfully. He came on the plane with me and delivered me to the facility.

Upon admission, I was searched, and my belongings were checked for drugs. I was quite familiar with that experience.

Before I transferred to the therapeutic floor, the admissions team reviewed the rules with me. Cell phones were prohibited. In fact, I wasn't to have contact with anyone on the outside for ten days.

I didn't like stupid rules. Later that day, I walked the halls, getting the lay of the land. Call it a little recon mission on my part in case I had to run or escape. I noticed a phone in an office and when I tried the door, it was open. I saw a window of opportunity to call my boyfriend. No harm, no foul.

I was on the phone for a while before I got busted. The staff kindly pointed out the rules also applied to me. I always thought rules were for people who could not figure a way around them or over them. That was my arrogance raising its ugly head. Pride and arrogance were two of my most destructive character defects. Not real pride, false pride. Always thinking I was secretly smarter than everyone else.

I had blood work done when I got to the detox floor. The following day I met with the doctor to go over the results. He introduced himself and asked me why I was there.

"I don't know, you tell me," I quipped. "You have the blood work."

Of course, I knew the blood work had come back clean because of my ten days of not using. Then I told him about the intervention and pleaded my case to him.

"Look, my family pulled an intervention on me, but I don't need to be here. I've already been on an opiate blocker for ten days, and I intend to stay on it. Plus, I really need to get home. My grandmother is in a nursing home recovering from surgery and she needs me. My father is around, but he's angry at my family for the whole intervention thing and doesn't want the burden of caring for his mother."

Truly, I felt torn. I wanted to please my mom and sisters but did not want to let my grandmother down or provoke my dad. What was best for me was not a consideration in my mind. It never had been. I was getting pretty old, and I had no idea what my purpose on earth was. I figured it was to make other people's lives more comfortable and manageable. I thought that was a higher purpose. I did not see the self-centeredness in my behavior for a few more years.

I didn't mention to the doctor that I also needed to get outta there because they had just charged $6,000 on my credit card for one week. Yes, one week. I was not about to go further in debt for my discomfort. That money would have bought a lot of stuff, not to mention that I wasn't worth the investment.

After the doctor and I talked for a bit, he said something I will never forget.

He said I looked like a hard-core addict.

I did not respond. I did not want to take the bait and get angry. After all, why should I care what these people thought of me? I knew I would never see them again. I was not concerned about my image or looking good.

Nevertheless, his words hit a nerve.

They reminded me of something a counselor in a previous rehab facility had said to me. She'd said that whatever my first thought was, I should do the opposite. Insulted and offended, I thought, *Who do you think you are?*

I did not understand that statement for years. Her comment finally made sense after I worked a recovery program. Then I finally understood.

Over the next several days, I attended groups and more groups. In one afternoon group, the leader asked all of us to share what is known as a trigger for using. People gave their reasons or excuses for drinking and drugging. Every excuse from "I don't get along with my parents" to "my wife is mean to me" was used.

Then it was my turn. What was my trigger for using?

"I woke up this morning and am breathing," I said. But as I said the words, something broke a little in me. The doc was right. I really was a hard-core addict with no one to blame but myself.

In another class, I heard statistics that did not bode well for me. Not many women my age were successfully staying sober. I was starting to see who I had become, but an important question remained: Was I willing to work to change that?

Unfortunately, the answer deep inside me was still no. A future without using scared me more than my current set of circumstances or pain.

One humid August afternoon, a group of us were outside smoking cigarettes and laughing at each other's jokes. This German guy decided to do a supermodel impersonation for us. He bent over, fluffed his hair, flung his head back, tied his T-shirt up over his belly, and strutted down the sidewalk like it was the catwalk. It was the funniest moment I'd witnessed there. But it wasn't humorous enough to make me want to hang around.

September was coming, which is the height of hurricane season in Florida. I needed to get home. I bugged the nurses about getting me an antidepressant the doctor had prescribed me. They told me they didn't know anything about it. Between that, the storm on its way to Florida, and not sleeping well at night, I was getting obnoxious and rude.

I had only been there five days.

One day, at three o'clock in the morning, I decided I was done. I was going home.

I walked to the nurse's station.

"Am I allowed to leave?" I asked, fidgeting.

"Of course."

I took a shower, packed my suitcase, and asked someone to call me a cab.

I still believed I could figure things out on my own—even though it was apparent to everyone but me that hadn't been true for years. My false pride was unbreakable. I still could not accept any help. How much worse would I get?

I had no cash, so I charged a seventy-five-dollar cab ride to an airport hotel. The first thing I did when I got to my room was call my mother. I dreaded that call but wanted her to know I was safe and on my way home to Florida.

I heard the pain and disappointment in her voice. She was heartbroken that I had left rehab.

I crawled between the cool, crisp hotel sheets with the big, fluffy pillow and took a very long nap.

The next morning, I took the hotel shuttle to the airport, got a flight, headed home. I was running away from looking in the mirror. I could not face myself, my shame, or my guilt. I did not know if I ever would.

I came home to all the same dysfunction and problems I left. After all, I had only been gone six days! I wanted to stay clean, so I stayed on the medicine. I figured that would take care of everything. I did not bother to go to any recovery meetings.

I did not change any of my behaviors. I hung around with users and drug dealers. I hated being alone and hated being home. I stopped speaking to my family. It was too painful for them and me.

There are three parts to a successful recovery: physical, emotional, and spiritual. I was like a cat on a hot tin roof. Emotionally and spiritually, I was empty. I thought things would have to get better because surely they could not get any worse. Boy, was I wrong.

Miserable and depressed, I lasted eight weeks without using opiates. If life was this empty, I did not care anymore. I was sober at this point, and if this was it, I was not interested in the effort it took to stay that way.

Naturally, I had heard of crack cocaine. That was the one drug I swore I would never try.

One day, after not using since before the intervention, I was on my way home from a pedicure and stopped by a friend's house to say hello. She and a drug dealer I knew were smoking crack. When they offered the pipe to me, I thought, *What the heck?* and hit it.

I had never been high like this before. You will give up everything you own, including your soul, chasing the feeling from your first hit. They call it chasing the dragon.

A few years after that experience, I spoke to that guy who gave me that hit, and he apologized to me. He knew me and was pretty sure I would take to the crack pipe like a baby to a pacifier. All he wanted was a new paying customer.

Well, he got what he wanted. I started to buy crack every day. I stayed up all night and watched TV and smoked. When staying home became a drag, I started staying out all night to smoke with other people.

There is a dark and scary world that wakes up after ten o'clock at night. It is spooky. I used to call it night crawling. There is nothing good happening on the street after that time. I often fought with my boyfriend about it. He searched me at times to see if I had dope hidden on me.

I did not care what he thought any longer. I wanted him to leave anyway so I would not be held back from doing exactly what I wanted when I wanted.

KELLY SPEAKS

I'd predicted to Bob that Karen would refuse to accept help, wreak havoc on the unit, and eventually check herself out. And that's exactly what happened. But there was no satisfaction in being right in this situation.

At the height of Karen's addiction, she would defiantly say how "free" she was and that no one could make her stop using or do anything that she didn't want to do. Because of her so-called freedom and dangerous, bizarre behaviors I began to think that Karen would be dead and buried any day now. I never thought anyone could come back from the darkness and despair of her addiction.

I didn't see a way out for our family, or a way to heal the pain and hopelessness that lingered.

15

Boundaries Are Easy to Set, Hard to Live By

KELLY SPEAKS

Karen continued to use for three more years. Things went from bad to worse.

As for me, I was caught in an unhealthy triangle, consisting of my mother, Karen, and me. I would speak to my mother daily, and we would ask each other the same questions repeatedly:

"Have you heard from Karen?"

"How did she sound?"

"What did she say?"

"Do you think she's using?"

"What kind of danger is she in?"

"What risks do you think she's taking?"

Mom spent many sleepless nights crying, praying, and begging for help. I didn't have the heart to tell her what I knew about addiction and the drugs Karen was using. I knew if she were using and selling crack cocaine and opiates, she was doing things we could never imagine. Afraid the knowledge might literally have killed her, I thought it was best if she didn't know.

I always took Karen's phone calls. Most of the time she called in hysterics, asking for help. I responded immediately and set up admissions to premiere treatment centers. After the third time, I got wise and suggested she be on the intake calls with me. I knew she needed to take the lead and take action in her own recovery journey. This fell on deaf ears and nothing happened.

My professional friends supported me and therefore supported my sister. I knew rationally no one held a grudge or judged my family or me, but I felt embarrassed and ashamed of her. I called in professional favors only to have them rebuked by Karen. I put my reputation on the line and felt extremely vulnerable after these situations. It wasn't about me, but it hurt my ego. I thought I could make a difference. Eventually, I retired my red cape and surrendered my savior complex.

Whether Karen called my mother or me, the topics were always the same.

She insisted her phone was bugged by the FBI and CIA. She believed her conversations were being recorded. She was going to take down the Deland drug dealers. She insisted that she couldn't talk long because the phones were causing brain cancer, and she didn't want to take the risk. She threw away disposable phones after each use.

In a way, the bizarre conversations were comforting because they validated that she was still alive. But have you ever tried having a meaningful conversation with someone in a drug-induced psychosis? It's crazy making! We tried to reason with her and have a linear discussion, but that was impossible.

The phone calls and conversations left us frantic. We anxiously waited and hoped to hear from her because there was no way to reach her.

The worst experience for my mother was when Karen called, wholly distraught, and said she had a gun and was going to shoot herself. Frantic, Mother called me and asked what we should do. But Karen moved from hotel to hotel, her home became a flophouse, and we did not know where she was. We were helpless to intervene.

I honestly thought that Karen was slowly but surely killing herself, and maybe shooting herself was a better alternative to the current hell she lived in. I know this is harsh. I know that thinking suicide is a better alternative to life is disgraceful. But I already had Karen dead and buried in my mind and didn't see any way she could possibly come back from her addiction. I thought her destructive behaviors would lead to certain death. How quickly she would die and the circumstances of her impending death were yet to be revealed.

It makes me sick to my stomach to admit this and to put it in writing. I wanted some relief for Karen and our family. I couldn't take the constant state of anxiety, panic, and desperation we felt over her addiction. I couldn't shoulder my family's burden anymore. I was tired. This was my bottom from enabling and codependent behavior.

Somehow, I needed peace from the daily chaos Karen caused our family. My family tried to reason, cajole, bribe, shame, guilt, and beg her to get help. I would have done anything to alleviate my mother's pain.

I realized that I had to start putting my own needs first. I had not gotten sober to experience the daily level of uncertainty, fear, and chaos she was causing in my life. I heard words like *boundaries, self-care, enabling,* and *codependency,* but how was I to begin? I was so busy trying to control and take care of other people's needs, I was unaware of my own.

So another "opportunity" for growth began.

I was ready to seek guidance and do something different. I learned to "detach with love," which sounded foreign to me. Having a family member addicted to drugs or alcohol caused me isolation. I admit it; I didn't go to work, social functions, holiday parties, or talk to colleagues about drug psychosis. On the contrary, I worked hard to look successful and composed on the outside so no one knew the loneliness and hopelessness I felt on the inside.

I needed to get some distance from Karen and the daily conversations I had with my mother. I didn't quite know how to accomplish this. I consulted with trusted friends and decided to set specific parameters regarding my sister.

My family's perception was that I was giving up and abandoning her if I limited contact. My mother and I would argue about my boundaries, and she did not support my choices. I gave my mom solicited advice about limiting contact with Karen so she could have peace in her life, but she wasn't emotionally willing to make the necessary changes.

I learned that neither of us was right. It's imperative that family members get help, whether it's through a twelve-step program, clergy, licensed professional, layperson, or a trusted friend. Each person needs to decide what they are willing to do and not do to assist the addict/alcoholic in their lives. How was it fair for me to tell my mom how to manage her daughter? Only she could make these decisions and wade through the choices that felt right for her. The same was true for me.

I set two boundaries that helped bring some peace and freedom into my life, whether Karen was using or not.

The first boundary was one I set with my mom. Throughout the years, my relationship with my mother had become all about Karen. I realized that I wanted my relationship with my mom back. My mom, sister, and I were in a codependent relationship. We did not know where one of us started and the other ended.

So when I told her that I was no longer willing to ride the roller coaster regarding Karen's drug use and addiction, I also told her that I missed her and wanted our relationship back. I asked her to respect my boundary and requested that all future conversations not include Karen. I told her that if I wanted to hear about Karen, I would ask her; otherwise, I didn't want to talk about her anymore. I explained I needed to do this to maintain my sobriety and sanity.

My mother didn't quite understand the request, but I also knew that she loved and respected me. I knew she was proud of my sobriety and wouldn't want to interfere with this. My mom listened!

This simple request changed the unhealthy dynamic between us. Our relationship flourished, separate from Karen.

The next significant boundary I set was to stop taking Karen's phone calls. I was no longer willing to engage in her psychotic rants. I knew that encouraging these conversations was counterproductive. I wrote a script to use when Karen called. First, I acknowledged it was good to hear from her and told her I loved her. Then I said, "Do you want help for your drug problem?"

You can imagine how this went over. The first phone call ended in my sister yelling profanities into the phone and denying she had a drug problem. She was enraged I would suggest such a thing.

The second call went pretty much the same way. I calmly said that I loved her and it was great to hear from her. Then I asked if she wanted help for her drug problem. She acted flabbergasted and denied having any trouble. I calmly informed her that I didn't think we had anything else to talk about, and we ended our call.

The third time was a charm. We went through the same script, but that was the last time Karen called me.

I struggled with my sense of guilt. At some level, I did think that I was abandoning my sister. The internal conflict was brutal. The judgment from my mom and other family members was harsh.

That said, the support that I got from trusted friends was invaluable. My goal was accomplished, which was to create some distance between my sister and family and begin to enjoy the life I had worked so hard to develop and that I deeply valued. I truly surrendered my sister's addiction to God and got out of the way. I realized I was not God.

What I want to express to you, dear reader, is that there are many ways to get to the same destination. No one can tell you the right way to handle a situation with a loved one who is an alcoholic or addict. However, they can give you ten ideas of ways to begin detaching with love or provide ways to set a boundary. Perhaps your heart will allow you to try two!

When I resolved that I had done what I could to intervene for Karen, and realized my actions added to the problem, I was able to let go of the outcome entirely. If Karen got sober, wonderful. If she died, I would be devastated. Either way, it was not up to me. Either way, I had the right to move forward with my life.

This was when I began to experience true freedom. Unfortunately, addiction and alcoholism can lead to death, which is traumatic for the loved ones left behind. What a miracle it is that Karen did get sober. Thank God she didn't kill herself. Thank God that He had other plans for her! The blessings that were in store for her were unimaginable! Never give up hope!

Here is a poem I wrote shortly after Karen's intervention. I think it provides a nice summary.

October 3, 2010
I drew a line in the sand.
To no longer stand
For the lies, manipulation, and pain
You have caused me.
I know you are sick, so I pray.
Pray for your best good.

Pray for your safety.

Pray for your health.

Pray for your sobriety.

For I know, I am helpless, powerless.

I'm grieving, for I have lost you.

My heart aches with such an acute sadness.

My mind wonders with care and concern.

I've lost my sister, for she is high on oxy, percs, and patches.

KAREN SPEAKS

Honestly, I had no idea my behavior was causing my family such anguish. I was lost in psychosis and conspiracy theories. I figured they were living their lives and enjoying their successes.

When I found out I was the subject of many distressed phone calls, I was not affected by their pain. I ignored it. I told myself I was protecting them from my ugly world.

Of course, that was a big lie.

The truth is that I did not want anyone to interfere. If I could have stopped for them, I would have. I loved them enough, I just didn't love myself enough.

16

I Wanna Meet a Fireman

KAREN SPEAKS

My worst fear came true. My grandmother's health deteriorated, and she passed away. I could not stay away from drugs long enough to be with her as she drew her last breath. Despite feeling grateful that my father was with her and she was not alone when she died, I was overwhelmed by grief and sorrow.

My family met in New Jersey for my grandma's funeral. My dad and I drove my grandmother's ashes back for burial. We were quite the deplorable pair. I made him drinks on the way, and I smoked dope right in front of him. What disgusting, disrespectful, pathetic behavior. Regardless of his behavior, I was wrong. He was my father, and for that alone he deserved respect.

When my mother and sisters saw me, they were shocked by my appearance. I was fifty years old and looked seventy. I was ninety-eight pounds and wearing a size three. I called it crack skinny. I thought it was cool. My extended family asked if I was sick or had cancer. I unabashedly asked my cousins to find drugs for me. I was out of my comfort zone and supply. I shamed and embarrassed my family.

I had an unusual experience while there. After the funeral, we hosted a luncheon. I passed a spot that interested me on the drive to the restaurant. I felt drawn to this place and turned in to park. It was a convent.

It was a gorgeous June day. The grounds were beautiful and the sun was shining on everything. I remember having a random thought about how great it would be to stay there in a motorhome for the summer.

I started looking around for a nun in a habit. I had serious questions about God, and I wanted answers. Like, where was He, and why was He letting me live like this? If He was supposed to be all that and a bag of chips, He should have changed my life by now. Maybe He was like the Wizard of Oz. A big fake.

Ladders and tools were lying around, but I couldn't find a single person. I knocked on the front door at the main house, but no answer. I badly wanted to go inside. I thought there would be some magic answer for me. Maybe this spiritual site offered easy instructions on how to change myself.

I decided I was not giving up yet. Perhaps I would check back later after the luncheon. Then I had another thought: If the door wouldn't open, I should try the window.

I opened a window from the outside. Lucky for me, it was not locked. After I crawled through the window, I stood, frozen, inside of the living room. I felt so peaceful. There was still nobody around. I was too scared to go exploring. What if I got caught? Just what I needed. I remember saying a prayer before I left, but I don't recall what I prayed. I loved the way that place felt. I wanted to stay there for a long, long time.

After the funeral, the drive back to Florida was sad. My grandmother had connected me to the rest of the family. I suspected that I had just seen some of my family for the last time. The area still felt like home, even after all these years.

My dad decided to go back to Grenada again. My boyfriend moved out while I was gone. Now, I was alone with my drugs. No grandmother, no dad, no boyfriend. Just me and the crack.

Now I had no responsibilities; nothing was holding me down. No anchor to reality at all. I went on a bender that lasted two additional years.

The local policemen knew me and my house because I was arrested a few times for drug possession. I was a nothing in their eyes. I lived in a small town, so you're an easy target once you are on their radar. They felt I got what I deserved. Maybe I did.

There were many police incidents. The first was a result of me calling the Fire Department.

I had just driven home from a few nights at a local dive hotel. I let myself in the front door, and the house was a mess. It was cluttered, dirty, and littered with homemade bongs and chore boy all over the place. Chore is used as a filter to smoke crack. One of my favorite things to do when I was high was to make creative smoking apparatuses.

I opened the door to air out the house. Suddenly, I got this idea that my house was going to catch on fire and spontaneously combust—despite the fact that I have no gas lines in my home. I thought there might be methane underground. I was deep into my psychotic thinking. I wanted to save my home.

My best thinking told me to call the fire department. Not the emergency number, of course, just the regular number. That is precisely what I did.

The dispatcher had difficulty understanding my concern since nothing was on fire yet. She said she would send someone anyway. True to her word, about forty-five minutes later a fire engine drove up with handsome, strong firemen coming to my door. They asked me a few questions, looked at each other strangely, then walked around the house. They said everything seemed fine, and I was satisfied with that.

When they started asking questions about the paraphernalia lying around, I used the "I don't know. It's not mine. I don't live here" excuse.

While I was waiting for them to leave, a sheriff's car pulled in the driveway. The firemen had ratted me out and called the police! I knew I was in trouble; this was not going to be good.

A cop came to the front door, and I told him he could not come in without a warrant. I knew I did not have to let him in. I got upset and combative. The next thing I knew, the cop came in anyway, looked around, and proceeded to throw handcuffs on me. He read me my rights and arrested me. I was shoved in the back seat of the cop car and transported to the Volusia County Jail.

I had just gotten myself arrested. This was totally on me. In fact, I had actually called them on myself. Who does that? That began my ongoing friendship with the bail bondsmen.

I called the cops a second time when someone close to me barged into my house and violently wrecked dishes and furniture. Afraid he would come back, I called the police.

When the law got to my house, they came in, surveyed the damage, looked at me, and said, "You ought to clean this shit up."

I cried out of frustration and anger.

The third time I called the police, I reported my car stolen. Unbeknownst to me, a friend had taken my car keys and traded my car for some dope.

If I'd hoped for help, I was wrong again. The police came to my house, took the report, and did nothing.

A few weeks later, I was riding along with someone else, and I saw my car driving through town. I said, "That can't be my car, can it?"

We tried to follow it, but it disappeared. I figured someone in my circle of friends knew the person who had stolen my car, but no one was talking. I got madder and madder by the day. Then I had an idea. If the police wouldn't help me, I would have to figure it out myself.

I sent a text to every dope dealer and druggie in my phone (and there were many) and offered two hundred dollars to anyone who got my car back, no questions asked. My car appeared in my driveway two days later. I was relieved to get it back and stuck to the bargain. Sticking to my word was always important to me, even when I was at my worst.

People in my neighborhood considered me a nuisance. I shared one of my delusions with my neighbor and explained I believed I had radiation poisoning. She acted concerned and suggested I visit the emergency room. I had a fear of hospitals, but for some reason, I went.

The look on the nurse's face was priceless when I told her I was there for radiation poisoning. They triaged me, and I waited on a cot in the ER hallway. I was so tired. As the nurse with the mobile cart arrived to gather information, a woman and man walked by me. The woman had a pack of cigarettes in her hand, which I noticed because I smoked the same brand.

She looked right at me and said, "It's all going to be okay, Karen."

She even used my name. There was no way this random stranger could have known my name. I freaked out.

I looked at the nurse. "Did she just say my name?"

The nurse confirmed that she had.

To this day, I believe in my heart that this stranger was an angel sent to comfort me during some of my deepest confusion. I never made any sense out of it, and it stuck with me for an awfully long time. I have never seen her again.

The ER nurse called in a shrink from the nut ward to consult with me. I caught on quick as he started asking me questions. Willing to do anything to stay out of another nut ward, I climbed off the gurney and tried to leave. The shrink continued asking questions, but I refused to answer and stated that if they couldn't give me answers about my radiation poisoning, I was leaving.

The tech came and drew some blood and sent it to the lab. In the meantime, they moved me to a small room. At least I was out of the hallway and not being gawked at!

I dozed off in the room until the doctor came in with the lab results. I was 100 percent certain about being poisoned. What else would give me all these strange symptoms? I had done homework ahead of time and spent hours asking Dr. Google to match my curious symptoms with possible diagnoses.

The doctor gave me the results. She assured me I had not been poisoned but had extremely high levels of cocaine in my system.

I told her that I certainly knew that. That was no surprise. I still wanted to know what was wrong with me. I refused to acknowledge I could be acting this way because of the drugs.

I started to think they might keep me there against my will.

While waiting for the discharge nurse, I simply took the IV out of my arm and walked out of there. As soon as I got home, a party buddy came by to get high. I never knew who would show up at my house and at what times of the day or night. There was no beginning and no end. I was still crazy, still using.

Where was my savior? I needed one indeed.

By the way, not all policemen were nasty. Some were kind. One told me I seemed like a nice lady and asked how I got wrapped up in all of this. Well, I *am* a nice lady. Looking back, I could blame many things for my predilection for drugs and alcohol; however, at fifty-two years old, these were old, lame excuses. Even *I* did not believe them anymore.

The truth is, I'd made horrible choices in my life and never took responsibility for any of them. I realized these choices and consequences were mine, but it seemed too late to care. I felt as if it would be too hard to change. I decided to take the position of "this is who I am." I had no idea this was a cop-out. I lost track of what it was like to recognize a problem, take responsibility for it, and make a change.

At some point, though, my attitude changed. I began to take responsibility for myself and my choices. I have to admit; it was long overdue.

I promise to continue my story, but I want to flash-forward to something that happened a few years into my recovery. I had an experience that created a stark contrast between who I had been and who I had become. Whenever I think of it, I am reminded of all the beautiful ways God works in our lives.

Here's what happened:

I needed to get clearance for volunteering at the county jail and needed to pick up some courthouse records. As I gave the clerk my name, I heard someone call out to me.

I turned around and saw a tall gentleman in uniform. He said, "You don't recognize me, do you?"

I realized this was one of the policemen who had arrested me—more than once. He was one of the kind ones. Embarrassed, I felt my face flush.

He told me I looked great, and he was glad to see I'd straightened my life out.

I will always remember that because it was a moment that healed something in me. I thanked him for his generosity of spirit.

Then I probably ruined the moment. I had to get a dig in about his buddies not being quite the same.

I wish I hadn't said that.

My excuse is that I was still new at being my better self.

KELLY SPEAKS

I've already mentioned that I got rambling, psychotic phone calls from Karen. Can you imagine trying to make sense of these incoherent conversations? These calls left my mother and me feeling absolutely frantic. We lived in constant fear and concern for Karen's safety and welfare. Karen's addiction brought us to our knees, and we knew we were defeated and helpless. Our solace was our prayers, but honestly, I was really pissed off with God. He seemed to be taking his sweet time rescuing Karen. She had to have all her freedoms taken away. She had to be arrested, detained, and mandated to long-term treatment by the courts before she would get help.

17

Jail House Rock

KAREN SPEAKS

I needed saving, and my savior came in an unusual way.

I was arrested again. I became an unenthusiastic guest of the Volusia County Corrections Department for three months in 2013.

I had always been able to bond out of jail. My bondsman was on speed dial. In the past, he had repeatedly gotten me released. He was nice to me and had gone as far as to take me home and get me McDonald's. That's the kind of service I'm talking about! It does not reflect highly on you or your social circle when you are a top referral source for the bail bonds company.

So, imagine my surprise when I called them from lock up, and they told me the judge had revoked my bond due to repeat offenses. This was a shocking wake-up call. Talk about sobering up fast.

I was granted three local phone calls. All my contacts were other drug addicts, so that wasn't helpful. The truth is, I had no one to call other than my mom, but that was a long-distance call, and I had no way to pay for this. I had burned all of my relationships and bridges. Thankfully, a kind social worker called my mother after orientation so someone in the world would know where I was. I was deeply concerned about my mom thinking I was dead in a ditch. She worried a lot about things like that—for good reason.

There is an expensive, complicated system to make phone calls from jail, and someone from the outside must set up an account. I am so grateful for my family in seeing me through this. They still loved me and sent money to me. It took over a week to get the phone account set up and ten days to get a candy bar from the commissary.

I received an inmate pamphlet and attended an orientation class about the rules. It is best to know the rules. Ignorance of the law is not an acceptable excuse. You cannot even get a bar of soap in jail if you have no money on your books. You do get a small starter pack like at a cheesy hotel. The "welcome pack" consisted of a small bar of soap, mini travel toothpaste, and a toothbrush with a one-inch handle so you could not stab someone. I was relieved when I got my own personal roll of toilet paper. I had no bra or underwear because when I was arrested, I wasn't wearing any. I should have listened to my mother's advice about always wearing a clean pair of underwear!

I felt so dejected. Here I was, fifty-two years old, confused, and in jail with a bunch of criminals. Yes, I said criminals! Not to mention, I had absolutely no plan or idea how to get out of the mess.

The jail was arranged in what they called blocks. It was a pod—four or five steel tables in an area surrounded by cells.

There were not enough cells, so the newbies, including me, slept on the floor in something called a boat. It was a canoe-shaped plastic structure with a thin mattress. You got two sheets that had been washed in bleach a thousand times, and you could see through them; they were paper-thin. I did not expect a luxury hotel, but really?

The temperature was freezing in there. Maybe this was purposeful to keep tempers from flaring, but this was Florida, and I was not used to cold temps.

When I noticed a few girls had two blankets, I begged for a second blanket but to no avail. When one of the girls was released, she gave me hers, and I was thankful. My fingers and toes were not numb that night. The first thing I ordered with my commissary money was socks. Oh, they felt so good—a pair of white athletic socks that came up to my knees.

The only thing to do there was read, but I could see nothing without reading glasses. Before I got my commissary order, people lent me theirs, but I hated to ask. I did not want to owe anyone anything. Again, I did not know all the rules.

For example, one girl got mad at me because I gave my food to someone instead of her, and she had let me use her glasses. After chuckling about this, I realized it was considered a real offense by the other inmates. Well, I learned that lesson.

After that, I didn't have a lot of trouble. I was older than most of the inmates and used the "I'm old enough to be your mother" line to keep them in check. I knew many of the girls from the drug scene around town. It registered in my brain that it probably was not such a good thing I recognized so many people. My innocent family had fears of me being beaten up and cowering in the corner. I was lucky they answered the phone when I called.

One night, I got a glimpse of the credits at the end of a TV show. The show was produced by a company that used the logo "Sit, Ubu, sit! Good dog!" Then they showed a license plate with their names on it. When I saw that license plate, it had Kelly's name on it. First and last name (Kelly Ryan). I knew it was a sign that my sister would be instrumental in helping me. I felt it in my spirit.

God was starting to show me things in many ways.

Kelly was also the liaison with my attorney. She communicated with him frequently. My other sister, Kolleen, was a doll and handled my bills for me. Even as they helped me, I was certain they must resent me because here I was again, making everyone's life harder while I lay around reading all day.

In the meantime, at my house, my crackhead friends were undoubtedly trashing my home and probably terrorizing my dog, Marty. I'd once caught them blowing smoke at his sweet little face and reacted furiously. He deserved better than that. I have forgiven myself for abandoning him. Even though it was not intentional, my actions still caused it.

Eventually, the cable and electricity got cut, so the squatters left my home.

I told one of the girls in my block this was probably the only time I appreciated my utilities getting cut off. She said something amusing back, and we started laughing so hard we were crying and could not stop. This was the first time I had genuinely laughed in years. I felt my brain starting to clear a little bit.

When my court date finally arrived, my attorney made a plea bargain with the judge. I got six months to one year of rehab and two years' probation. I was thrilled because, with three felony drug charges and some misdemeanor paraphernalia charges, I could have been sentenced to a prison term.

I had seen many of the girls on my block come back from court with prison sentences. Most were well deserved. One of my block mates was featured on the TV show "Snapped." Once, she asked me if I thought you could ID a person from just a toe. I figured you could with DNA and told her so.

I waited in jail until a bed became available at the county rehab facility. Rehab was part of my plea agreement. I managed to convince my attorney to get me out before I checked into rehab so I could take care of some business. If I were going to be there for six months, I would have to make arrangements.

Begrudgingly, he agreed, but only with the condition that I go to the courthouse every day for a urine test. I had nothing to lose, so I thought this was great. I heard words that were music to my ears: "Burd, pack it up."

I swore to myself I wouldn't use again, but that made no difference. The crack pipe found its way to my mouth on its own. I did go to the courthouse every day for my urine tests. I knew they were dirty, so I tried a few tricks. One was purchasing clean urine from someone, putting it in a tube, and putting it inside of myself. Truly desperate and disgusting behavior. An attendant observed me through a small window while I did the UA. I was so nervous, I messed up my plan and got caught. I was surprised they did not take me into custody right there as I ran out of the building.

My attorney notified me of my new court date. He stated I would be in jail for one night, then transferred. I started getting high and decided I did not need to show up in court. I entertained the idea of leaving the area and going on the run. I was now a fugitive in my delusional world who needed to get out of dodge. I lasted about three days before getting caught and arrested again with new charges and warrants from the no-show case.

I was in serious trouble this time, and I was scared. Back to county jail I went. Not much had changed since the previous week. My attorney told my sister he was going to drop my case unless I paid another $8,000. Reason being? I had not complied with the plea deal; therefore he had to begin the process all over again. I had plenty of money in the bank, but it wasn't doing me any good where I was, so why not pay it? Fine by me.

The only time I ever thought about God was when I wanted something from Him. I never asked what I could do for Him. As I was praying, *Dear God, give me my life back*, I realized what had passed for a life for many years was an empty existence. I realized I did not want it back. Nothing that I ever thought would make me happy did. Not my home, not a relationship, not the success from work, not my bank account. Absolutely nothing.

Another level of surrender flushed through my brain and body. I no longer cared what I could have back or hold onto from my old life. I saw a small sliver of hope that I might have a new life, one that was worth living. I did not know how to get there, but I was beginning to believe that it was possible.

In fact, seeds of belief had been planted a few months earlier, before my arrest, with an experience one night in my backyard pool. I didn't tell anyone about this for a while because I was afraid they would accuse me of being high or crazy. Of course, I was both of those things, but that didn't change my experience.

On a clear, warm summer night, I'd been floating in the pool when I'd looked up and saw a cross made of stars in the night sky. Immediately, a profound sense of peace flooded my spirit, and I'd known in my heart and in every cell of my body that I would be okay.

Jesus had met me where I was that night. Since that moment, I had wanted to know Him better. I wanted that sense of peace again. Like the real alcoholic I am, I wanted more of anything that felt good.

By the grace of God, when my new court date came around, I ended up with the same plea deal. I knew God was watching over me.

This time, I had to wait for a new bed to become available in rehab. Time ticked by as I waited another five weeks in jail.

In jail we had headcount four times a day. We stood in front of our cells, all tucked in, as a matter of procedure. One day, during headcount, we waited for the officer and the end of *The Ellen DeGeneres Show* was on TV. Bruno Mars was singing a song called "When I Was Your Man." I was watching the faces of the girls react to his beautiful lyrics. It was never quiet in jail, but at that moment, you could have heard a pin drop.

I saw past all the girls' coarse and tough exteriors and saw the pure, beautiful spirits inside each woman there. My heart broke for them and for me.

I decided Ellen should know about this, so should Bruno Mars. After all, it was his song. I wrote a letter to Ellen to describe this moment in time and thank her. I fantasized about being a guest on her show one day and relating this experience. I knew she would get in touch with me after reading my letter. Fast-forward . . . I have not heard from her yet.

My thinking became institutionalized. Having no expectations and a boring daily routine made me complacent. I didn't
have to make any decisions at all in jail. I had all my necessities, a roof over my head, and three squares a day. In fact,
sometimes I thought that if I got to be seventy-five and ran out
of money, I could rob a bank and come back here. All my needs
would be met, and I'd have friends to play cards with all day
long.

The girls knew the breakfast, lunch, and dinner menus
by heart. Beans, beans, beans. It is a good thing that I like
beans. They were the staple of our diet. By the way, jail tricks
get passed down from inmate to inmate, but it was all new to
me. Let me tell you, MacGyver had nothing on these girls. They
sculpted eyebrows with thread and made eyeliner out of pencil
dust. And the desserts they made from commissary items were
amazing. My favorite treat was iced honey buns and snicker
bars.

I had endless time to reflect about who God is. That tends
to happen in jail. One girl told her dad that God was always with
her when she was in prison, and he asked her why she didn't
bring Him home with her. Good point!

I started to read the Bible from the beginning. I thought this
was a productive way to spend my time. I heard one of the girls
quote a scripture about fear, and it blew my mind. The scripture
was 2 Timothy 1:7. It reads, "For God has not given us a spirit
of fear, but of power and of love and of a sound mind." That is
my favorite scripture and the first one I ever remembered.

It dawned on me that I had always been afraid. I acted
tough but was secretly a marshmallow on the inside. I realized
I had been paralyzed by my past failures and fear of the future.

I wondered what it would be like to have a spirit of power, love, and a sound mind as described in the Bible. Was that even possible?

A sliver of light broke through—a little light and a little hope.

There were girls on my block who were there for armed robbery, and two or three were charged with murder. And yet I sat with these women and had Bible study at night in our cells. Human beings are magnificently complicated creatures. The thought amazed me that a person who could share a cupcake with you could also murder her mother.

Sometimes Christian volunteers visited the jail. At first, I would go to the services and classes to get out of the block, but that began to change. I knew by now that God was real, but if I surrendered to Him, what would that mean? How would I go about this new life I was being offered?

I looked forward to the rare treat of going outside. We lined up in the hallway and had to be super quiet, but when the door opened and I walked into the beautiful sunshine, my arms went automatically up toward the sky. I believe it was my praise position because I would say out loud, "Thank you, God."

I was still waiting to be admitted to rehab. I considered trying to be open-minded about rehab instead of fighting it every step of the way. I had a massive chip on my shoulder. I thought if God were going to fix me, it should be like magic. Wrong. Magic is an illusion; God is real. I grew open to the idea of listening to others.

After all, I had seen where my big ideas and grand plans had gotten me. I let myself want something more from life.

On November 9, I heard those words again: "Burd, pack it up." A woman had arrived to transport me to Rehab.

I was frightened but ready.

KELLY SPEAKS

In October 2013, my mom received a call from a guard at the county jail, notifying her that Karen had been arrested and was being held without bail. The guard explained that by calling Mom she was breaking the rules, but she was doing it because she was a mother herself.

She described Karen as being in a vulnerable position, crying hysterically and begging someone to notify her mother that she was safe. To this day, I am thankful for the compassion the guard showed toward our family—particularly our mother.

My sisters, stepfather, and I were devastated when Mom called to notify us about the current situation and arrest. We didn't think she had the strength to manage the environment, and imagined every horrific scenario in our heads. What if she were raped or beaten? Or became suicidal and was found dead in her cell?

When the initial shock wore off, we realized these were unsubstantiated fears. We experienced relief knowing Karen was safe in a cell instead of on the streets using drugs. For the first time in years, my mom got a decent night's sleep.

My sisters and I searched online for Karen's public arrest record. When we found her mug shots, we were horrified and shocked to see how spaced out and high she looked.

Reading public records on her, we discovered that she had been arrested twelve times previously. We had no idea!

"We can't show this to Mom," I told my sisters. "It'll kill her."

Our intentions were to protect her. Looking back, though, we didn't have the right to withhold information or insulate her from reality. We eventually agreed to share the photos.

Karen's lawyer worked out a deal with the courts for her to go to a long-term rehab facility. He convinced the judge to allow her to leave

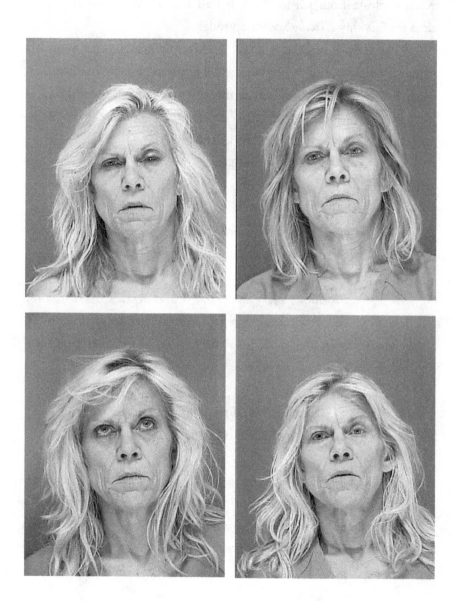

jail for a week to get her "affairs" in order. He arranged and supported Karen's release from jail to check herself into rehab voluntarily. Who does that? Is this a *Twilight Zone* episode?

I have since realized she was highly manipulative yet probably somewhat sincere. Maybe she even had intentions of going to treatment. Maybe, maybe not. Regardless, to me, the whole thing seemed ridiculous. How does someone get arrested twelve times for repeated offenses and continue to escape any consequences?

On October 11, 2013, the lawyer e-mailed these words to our family:

I feel somewhat responsible for Karen being released for a week before her inpatient drug treatment as a condition of her probation.

As a result of Karen being incarcerated and detoxed, I believed she would be able to stay drug-free for the week and get her affairs in order. I was mistaken. As a condition of her release, she was to be drug tested daily until she was sentenced.

Karen remained clean for less than twenty-four hours.

A few days later, he e-mailed us again:

I am afraid I have some bad news. I have not seen the latest police reports, but it appears Karen has been charged with new offenses occurring at the time of her latest arrest. They are fleeing and attempting to elude, possession of cocaine, paraphernalia, and driving while her driver's license is revoked.

If I continue to represent Karen, my fee for this case and the additional work on her behalf, is $8,000. Karen's new sentencing date is now set *on 11/7, but these latest charges may delay those proceedings. In light of Karen's failure to follow my instructions and the additional work she has caused me, I consider withdrawing from her cases.*

I cannot continue to represent her without additional compensation. If Karen can pay the fee, I will continue to represent her; otherwise, I feel I have no choice but to ask the court to withdraw from her representation.

After reading his e-mail our family agreed to his request, rallying to pay additional funds to the lawyer.

I was furious how Karen's circumstances continued to control my mother and family. I would have done anything to relieve my mother's pain, fears, and concerns, but how could I do this and be true to myself?

Wow, it was hard! I decided I was willing to be the point of contact with Karen's lawyer for the family. I had the skill set to do this, and it might be helpful to Karen. I was unwilling, however, to put money in her commissary, pay her bills, or manage her finances while she was in jail. I knew she had money, and I wanted her to feel the financial burden of the lawyer's fees and any other consequences that occurred.

I got counsel from a friend who served six years hard time in prison. He told me a pair of shower shoes and cigarettes could go a long way. I eventually changed my mind and contributed to Karen's commissary account. My purpose was to relieve my mother's financial burden. I knew she was spending money she didn't have to help Karen.

We learned a lot of information we did not want to know. During Karen's incarceration, my youngest sister was willing to be power of attorney and handle her outstanding bills. Our mother was Karen's main point of contact. I told my mom I would be happy to write Karen, but she would have to initiate the first contact. These were some of the boundaries I set to protect myself in order to have peace around Karen's incarceration. Per her lawyer's request, I wrote a letter to the judge requesting treatment instead of containment in prison.

September 17, 2013

Dear Court:

I am writing in regards to Karen Burd, Booking #9XXXXX. I am Karen's sister and am also a licensed marriage and family therapist. I've been licensed and working in the mental health and substance abuse field since 1996. I am in recovery and have been sober for eight years, and I actively work a 12-step program. My family has asked that I write a letter appealing to the court to mandate long-term residential drug rehabilitation for Karen. Long-term drug treatment is defined as a minimum of six months.

Karen has been a drug addict and alcoholic since her teen years. She has recently been in a drug-induced psychotic state, given her chronic use of crack cocaine. Without a treatment intervention, Karen will undoubtedly continue to be at risk to herself and the community at large. She will end up dead and possibly harming others along the way. She has lost any moral compass, given her addiction and need to get high. Our family is not in a financial situation to be able to afford treatment. We ask that the court consider mandating a treatment intervention, offering assistance rather than containment.

If Karen is released on probation, she will continue to break the law and harm herself and others. Our family has tried everything possible to help Karen get treatment. She has continuously denied any problem as well as gotten verbally abusive to her loved ones. Karen has tried and failed outpatient drug rehab endless times.

A thirty-day program is not enough time to make an impact with Karen. Long-term drug treatment mandated by the courts is Karen's best option to save her life. I realize that jail is not designed to provide treatment. Given Karen's arrest record and history, she will surely offend again, and prison becomes a revolving door with continued recidivism.

Again, we appeal to the court to mandate a long-term drug treatment center. Thank you for your consideration.

With Gratitude,
Kelly Ryan, LMFT (Sister)
Rosemarie Hinkle (Mother)
Jerry Hinkle (Step-Father)

At the same time, I wrote a letter for the attorney to take to the court concerning Karen's psychiatric and drug history:

October 14, 2013

Dear Lawyer:
As requested, I'm writing a history of Karen Burd's psychiatric, alcohol, and drug abuse history. Karen has an above-average IQ and was a straight A student through eighth grade. Our father is/was an alcoholic, and our home was often chaotic and unpredictable. He was violent when drunk, and Karen, as the oldest sibling, got the brunt of these physical attacks as well as my mother.

Karen had her first psychiatric hospitalization at age sixteen. This was around 1977. It was typical to have children admitted and stay in residential treatment long term. Karen was admitted into Northwest Community Hospital located in Arlington Heights, Illinois, for taking over-the-counter medications in the family's medicine cabinet. While at NWCH, she broke a light bulb and tried to slit her wrists. At this time, she was transferred to Old Orchard Hospital in Skokie, Illinois. Her most extended hospitalization was at Lakeshore Hospital in Chicago, Illinois, which lasted through her eighteenth birthday. She was in psychiatric hospital facilities or residential treatment for two years and completed high school while in the hospital. Even though Karen was in a locked and secure setting, she was able to run away, which resulted in the police finding her and bringing her back to Lakeshore Hospital. She got marijuana into the unit and was highly resistant to treatment.

She was able to come home for weekends and extended home visits. She had multiple episodes of running away, getting drunk, smoking pot, and was oppositional overall. Karen had a history of self-harm and burned her arms with cigarettes, leaving terrible scars. The most severe time was when she told my mother she had gotten burned by a motorcycle pipe. The burns were deep and had a circumference of about two inches.

During this period, her treating psychiatrist tried different types of psychotropic medications. Karen gained a lot of weight and felt drugged. As a teenager, this was devastating. She began refusing the medication and was noncompliant. There were multiple diagnoses and never any real clarity about what mental health issues were the primary concern. Karen has been diagnosed bipolar by most psychiatrists that she has ever seen. This has been a consistent theme since adolescence. Karen's mental health condition has been exacerbated by her chronic drug and alcohol use. At this time, Karen has been in a drug-induced state of psychosis. Karen is an alcoholic and drug addict. She began using alcohol during her adolescence and has a history of blackout drinking. She has had multiple DUIs, car accidents, and self-harm episodes while drunk. At age thirty, Karen had a DUI and stopped drinking. She has been in and out of the rooms of twelve-step programs for many years. The family thought she was sober but later realized that she was smoking marijuana and abusing benzodiazepines. Her disease progressed to using prescription medications, opiates, and, over the last couple of years, crack cocaine. She has continuously lied and stolen from family members. There have been many emotional breakdowns and brief periods of abstinence for Karen. I can't recount how many times family members have tried to help by providing support, refuge, and intervention. As a professional in the recovery field, I set up treatment interventions on three occasions because Karen called me and asked for help. She always changed her mind and didn't go. In August 2010, our family was concerned about her opiate addiction and hired an interventionist. We all flew to Florida. She was in treatment with Addiction Psychiatrist William Leach, MD, and was prescribed Suboxone. She was abusing and selling this drug. She went to a treatment facility in Houston, Texas, but checked herself out within five days.

Over the last three years, we have seen Karen spiral down and live a life as an addict and street person. As a result of her drug use, I believe she has been in a drug-induced psychosis. She is not of sound mind. There is nothing more painful for a mother, sister, and father than to watch the deterioration of someone's spirit due to drug addiction and mental illness. Over the years, we have witnessed a bright, successful, compe-

tent woman turn into a psychotic drug addict with all of the issues this infers: theft, lies, abuse, and incomprehensible demoralization.

It is a contradiction to expect an addict to stay sober on their own volition with this type of history. Karen has had mental health problems and polysubstance abuse all of her life. Our family prays that the courts provide long-term treatment rather than containment. If I can provide any additional information, please feel free to call me at 303 520-XXXX.

With Gratitude,
Kelly Ryan, LMFT

We all get to make choices. I got sober to be free of the daily chaos drinking caused in my relationships. I didn't want to be enmeshed with Karen or other family members who lived in her nightmare.

Because of that, I practiced and enjoyed the freedom in setting boundaries. It took courage to look in the mirror and realize the only person I control is me. I am not responsible for anyone else's feelings or reactions. If I set a boundary, the only person that must respect it is me. Setting and maintaining limits empowered me. Setting boundaries created opportunities for me to allow others to make their own decisions and blaze their own trail.

Our family agreed that appealing to the court was the best way to support Karen. I advocated for her and the court-mandated long-term treatment! Our family was cautiously optimistic. We recognized this as an immense opportunity and gift to Karen. What she would do with it was up to her. Our family had completed our work.

18

Karen Goes to Rehab

KAREN SPEAKS

Sitting in the transport van, I desperately needed a cigarette. I hadn't smoked for three months. I tried to bum one from the transport driver, but she didn't smoke.

Luck upon luck, we had to pick up another girl from detox to transport to rehab. As the van was idling outside the detox center, I asked the driver if I was allowed to leave the car for a minute.

"Sure honey, you're not in jail anymore."

I was elated by my newfound freedom. As soon as I was outside, I bummed a cig from a couple of guys loitering outside the detox center. Angel trumpets sounded in my head. I got my cig and smoked it. I didn't realize it would be my last for a while. I would soon find out the rehab where I was heading was non-smoking. It must have been the only non-smoking rehab on the planet.

This rehab center served many drug-addicted women with small children who had been reported to Department of

Children and Family Services. As I would soon learn, many of these women were working on getting their children back from foster care. Unfortunately, some mothers had their parental rights permanently terminated. If I did not harden my heart, it would break, watching the lives of their young children destroyed.

I had gained twenty pounds in jail from snacking on those honey buns. The Department of Corrections stored my clothes while I wore the fashionable orange jumpsuit assigned to inmates. It's a good thing orange was my color. My jeans were so tight when I was released that the button and zipper wouldn't close. My honey buns had turned into muffin tops!

Most of the staff at the rehab were kind. I'll never forget one woman nicknamed Miss Queenie. She was an elderly black lady with a huge heart and gentle spirit. She sat at her station reading her Bible and playing worship music. She gathered up clothing that fit me, a hygiene package, and washed my dirty clothes.

It had been some time since anyone had been nice to me. I cried at her humble gesture of kindness. Then I broke down into gut-wrenching sobs. I was so befuddled. How could this be my life? I was resident grandma to twenty-year-old street girls. Then it struck me, I was no better than any of them and fit right in. I was worse than those I was judging because they had youth on their side. I did not.

Did that mean I hadn't learned anything in the last thirty-some years of my life? Who did I think I was? How did I get this way? Looking back, I realized my false pride and extreme arrogance were beginning to crumble. Humility started to creep in.

The next morning, I went to breakfast and got a real cup of coffee. I was grateful for that hot, fresh cup of coffee; it tasted wonderful.

For any changes to occur in rehab, I knew I had to face some ugly truths about myself. Truths I had been running from for an awfully long time. Believe it or not, I was still not sure I was ready or willing to do this. I hyperventilated due to fear. Sometimes I thought I should forget the whole thing, go back to jail, and do my time.

There was one reason I did not do that. I was afraid I would be sentenced to prison. I was more fearful of prison than I was of looking at myself. Now that the choice was made, the question was, *Am I going to pass the time or make an effort at recovery?*

I decided I had nothing to lose. If I did not stay sober, nothing would be different anyway. I knew in the pit of my stomach this was my last shot. I decided to look at my opportunity for positive change instead of focusing on old, tired excuses.

Wow, what a difference when you change your perspective. The State of Florida was paying the tab for a chance at real treatment. How could I waste that? I previously used the ridiculous cost of treatment as an excuse to avoid getting sober. Now that excuse was off the table. The fact that my treatment was court ordered meant I could not leave. So, running, was not an option. I was now as ready as I would ever be for treatment.

I met my counselor the next day. I remember thinking, *I hope I don't get some twenty-five-year-old telling me what to do.*

Well, that was exactly what I got. I had more years conning the mental health system and experiencing drugs and alcohol

than she had been alive. I thought our sessions would be useless. My ego, pride, and judgement thwarted my ability to be
open to the process. I was running from myself for years and
had no idea where to start. I didn't know who I was separate
from my identity as a drug addict. I wanted to control my program and assignments.

In one session I said, "Look, just give me a list of everything
required to complete the program, and I'll do it on my own."

"No, it doesn't work like that," she explained. "I'll decide
when you can move forward."

Her words threatened my desire for control, and my supe-
riority complex was activated.

I still did not realize I was not in charge of any of this.

"Karen," she said, "you need to slow down and trust the
process."

There was one thing I started to understand: I knew absolutely nothing about living sober. Then it occurred to me: How
could I do something I did not know how to do? Well, I couldn't.
I was just never taught these things. I forgave myself a little bit
at that moment.

Every week a wonderful couple came to the facility and
ran a weekly Bible study. I had started to read the Bible when I
was in jail. I now knew who Jesus was and was curious to find
out what it all meant. I was seeking. I began attending the Bible
study and asking questions.

I had many realizations when doing my assignments.
There was a lot of writing and reading to do and a lot to process
during therapy sessions.

A massive surprise to me was that I had chosen my lifestyle. I had never even considered that notion! My entire life I

thought I was reacting to the actions of other people. I did not know I had choices. I know that sounds ridiculous, but it was true.

Another assignment was to write a goodbye letter to my drug of choice. I laughed out loud. My drug of choice was avoidance of my life. Any substance that got me there faster and more intensely would do, and I had run out of new drugs to try.

I understood my recovery and healing must go deeper than that or I would never stay sober. I decided to write a goodbye letter to the pain. Pain is what I wanted gone. Just thinking about this stuff made me feel like I had no skin on my body. If you touched me, I would scream like a banshee from sheer horror. I was that vulnerable. I felt like I was walking around naked in front of the entire world with no place to hide. Shame and guilt engulfed me. I understood why Adam and Eve hid from God after eating the forbidden fruit.

I had always caved and relapsed when I was forced to face my pain. Lucky for me, in rehab I was confined with nowhere to run. There was no sugarcoating this situation.

Oh my God, this was far more challenging than I had feared. Now I knew why my counselor would not give me all my assignments at once. It was impossible to get anything out of rushing through the work. My habit was to give up when reality got too overwhelming.

Have you ever heard the saying that the only way to eat an elephant is one bite at a time? That is exactly how I had to approach recovery, but it was not in my nature to do anything bite by bite. I found out that impatience was one of my biggest problems. Impatience was a part of my imperfect human nature.

Wow, another revelation.

I was just a human being like everybody else. Why should I expect more from myself than I expected from others? What a relief that thought was. My facade cracked a little more. I was not a piece of garbage, unworthy of breath unless I pleased someone else. I was just another person facing life. I didn't have to be more than or less than anyone. I could just be me, if I only knew who that was.

We did an exercise that visualized a man walking up twelve steps. The bottom step said false beliefs; the top step said freedom. I had to unlearn my false beliefs about everything to make room for something new. It was a hard pill to swallow when I realized I had been wrong and confused about so much, despite the fact that my counselor told me it was okay to be wrong and that I didn't need to have an answer for everything.

She assured me there I would find relief in being able to say "I don't know."

I couldn't believe that. You mean I did not have to prove how valuable and worthy I was to the world? She told me to trust the process, but what *was* the process? That made me furious. Is it some secret I don't know about? Please, someone, tell me.

No one gave me a satisfactory explanation, and I wanted an answer now. I always wanted to know how and why things worked. "Why?" had always been my favorite question. Why should I do that? Why shouldn't I do that? I thought that if I knew the inner workings of how and why, I could mentally rearrange the process to suit me.

Eventually I learned that my questions were really related to manipulation. And here I thought I was just extremely skilled in the art of persuasion!

I was beginning to scratch the surface of my recovery.

Living at the rehab center was like living in a dorm for bad girls. Our little sorority got dramatic. There was lots of catty bickering going on. It could be over someone eating an extra snack or a perceived dirty look. It cracked me up.

My false belief was that any woman who'd had a child taken away due to addiction just didn't love her kid enough. I didn't have children, so it was easy for me to judge; I had not walked in their shoes.

But what I witnessed there changed my mind. Most of these mothers loved their children deeply. But their disease came before everything. It was that powerful.

Every Sunday, we had a house meeting to get our assigned chores for the upcoming week. My favorite chore was kitchen cleanup. The cafeteria was one of the noisiest places I had ever been. There were two shifts for dinner. The kids and babies ate dinner with their mothers. It was more like a zoo than a dining hall due to the crying, whining, and throwing of food.

The kitchen setup was impressive, like a professional restaurant kitchen. Believe it or not, I enjoyed dish washing duty. The dishes would stack up high at the pass-through window as the girls dropped them off, and I would spray and rinse them one by one before putting them into the colossal dishwasher. The dishes came out spotless in minutes.

To me, a good production line is like a choreographed dance. Cleaning things made me feel good. Somehow it felt as if I were being cleaned.

One afternoon after doing the lunch dishes, I noticed a pot that had been sitting out for a couple of days. I looked inside, and it was gross. It was burned badly on the bottom, still mushy in the middle with a layer of scum on the top. I thought to myself, *They should toss this mess out and buy a new pot. This thing will never get clean.*

Reluctantly, I put my hand right in that mess and skimmed all the junk off of the top. It came right out. Then I dumped the middle out. That was easy, too, but I wanted to quit when I saw the bottom of the pot. The task seemed impossible, but it was my assigned chore. I scrubbed with a lot of elbow grease and a good, hard sponge. When I rinsed the pot, I started to see the bottom.

Now it was war. I was going to get this thing clean, even if it took me all day.

I scrubbed and scrubbed and rinsed and rinsed until finally, all that was left at the bottom of the pot was some stain that permeated the metal. The pot had been restored and looked better than ever!

Chefs claim that over time, a seasoned pot creates the most refined taste. What initially seemed beyond repair, through time and care, performed at its highest and best use.

It took thirty seconds for that entire thought to pass through my brain. I knew it was a sign from God mirroring my recovery journey. If I did the hard work step by step, process by process, I could be shiny and new. Remember how to eat the elephant? One bite at a time.

That moment gives me joy to this day. I did not have to be thrown out and discarded like the old pot. I wasn't useless. I shared this story with a friend years later, comparing the stain in the metal to the human stain in all of us. I turned my human stain over to God and asked to be a better person. So far, my pot is looking good.

My first holiday in rehab was Thanksgiving. I had settled in and felt actual gratitude on that day. I remember thinking I was one of the lucky ones. That was a significant change of attitude for me. Many of the girls got day passes to be with their families. I could have felt sorry for myself for being locked up over the holidays, but I was done with all the self-pity. Oh, poor me, poor me, pour me another drink. The caked-on part of that pot was like my self-pity. My thinking had to change, but I still did not know how to change it. To change my thinking, I had to first change my actions. My counselor had instructed me to focus on doing the next right thing. Okay, I could try that.

When Christmas came around, staff and local organizations made it nice for us. The mothers and their kids were excited. Me, not so much, and I admit that some self-pity crept in. My mother was so sweet; she sent lots of gifts and made cookies for me.

We would devour anything sweet because we had very little sugar in our food. We did not have access to candy or cakes. I created a candy smuggling system for myself. I had a credit card for doctor's appointments and other necessities that was held by the office staff. Whenever I had a doctor's appointment, the aid who drove me always waited in the van. After my doctor's appointment, on my way back to the van, I would sneak into a small café in the building, buy a bunch of candy bars, and smuggle them back for my roommate and me. I would come up with ailments to get some candy. A girl has to have some chocolate, right?

On Christmas Day I was allowed an unsupervised pass for the first time. My only friend agreed to pick me up for a few hours on Christmas Day. She got my car from my attorney, who got it out of impound. She was also keeping my sweet dog, Marty, for me. I swear, thinking of that little guy kept me going sometimes. I can only imagine how people feel about children if I feel like that about a dog.

She and her son had been my party buddies. I knew they had not changed, so I was a little scared. Truthfully, I was petrified. So we wouldn't have to spend time at her house, I bought her family of seven dinner at IHOP for Christmas! What? IHOP?

After dinner, they wanted me to score some drugs for them, but I refused.

I could not wait to get back to the safety of rehab. The temptation was tremendous, but I realized I had come this far and did not want to go back to the same way of life.

By God's grace, I got back clean. I surrendered a large chunk more of myself to God that night. I cried with relief when I returned and noticed a little more of my hard exterior had melted off.

My time at rehab was coming to an end. I had completed my six-month program in three and a half months and was being discharged early because they desperately needed beds for girls waiting in jail.

I was excited and frightened. I understood that staying clean on the outside was a "whole 'nother level." Staying clean was easy when your world was controlled and safe, but it's not like that in the real world.

When I was released, the friend I had spent Christmas with had been staying at my house for several weeks. I felt like she had replaced me in my own life. I had a lot to straighten out as soon as I got home, and I prayed for the courage to do so.

Her son was supposed to pick me up at 9:00 a.m. on discharge day. I waited, paced, and said goodbye to everyone. I felt like I kept saying goodbye over and over.

When he didn't show up, I was furious. By 11:45 a.m. one of the aides offered to give me a ride home. I put my stuff in the van.

We stopped at a convenience store for cigarettes and a Coca-Cola. It was the best cig and soda I ever had. It was stupid to start smoking again after seven months of not smoking, but I could not help myself. I had to give up everything else, and I was not ready to give up smoking.

I decided to live. I wanted a life. In the past, I had begged God to give me my life back. Now I knew I did not want my old life back. I was no longer afraid of the future because I had finally started to build faith and hope. Hope was a magnificent new feeling for me.

When I arrived home, my car was in the driveway, and my friends were passed out on the furniture. They had forgotten to get me.

Suddenly, a feeling of gloom and doom overtook me.

Who am I kidding? I thought in despair. *I am never going to be able to do this.*

Without a second thought, I had dashed my own hopes of sobriety. I asked my friend where she was keeping the bottle. She gave me a funny look, then handed it to me. I proceeded to get drunk. I had not been home for ten minutes, and I failed again.

I looked at the bottle in my hand.

I couldn't believe I was drinking!

Frantic, I managed to get a ride to the local AA meeting. I entered the meeting drunk and reeking of alcohol. I went outside after a few minutes because I thought I was going to vomit. It was the first poison I had put into my body in seven months. My body desperately wanted it purged.

Two people from the fellowship came outside and asked what they could do to help. They gave me a ride home, and I passed out immediately. I woke up a few hours later, in the middle of the night, with the awful realization I had gotten drunk. What now?

You would think I had learned my lesson after seven months of lockup. If I were to begin a sober life, I certainly could not do it living with two active addicts. I had to tell my friends to go. Telling them to go was one of the hardest things I have ever done. My nature was to be a people pleaser at my own peril. I had to change that. It was a huge victory for me to stand up for myself.

I went to an AA meeting that night and shared what I had done. I asked a woman I knew if she would sponsor me. Sponsorship means to guide me through the program and twelve steps. She said yes and told me to call her on my way home.

"Why should I call you on my way home?" I asked, puzzled. "We're talking now."

"Do it," she said, smiling.

I shrugged and answered, "Okay." And I did.

I know now she was testing me to see whether I was willing to take direction. I was more willing than ever.

This time, I was choosing life.

19

One Large Cup of Coffee, Please

KAREN SPEAKS

Being home alone was a new experience. I did not know where to begin. The outside porch was filthy. The grass was at least a foot tall. I tried to use some of my new thinking tools. I figured I could not get everything cleaned up in a day like I wanted to, so I would do what I could—day by day.

I surveyed my home. Many things were gone.

My television had been stolen. I figured my friends probably pawned it for drugs. Any piece of jewelry that meant anything to me had been stolen. My grandmother had given me her engagement ring, and I loved it. The diamond was purchased in Greece by a relative. The setting was created and designed just for her. It was a gorgeous, round, carat-and-a-half solitaire set in a platinum band. The monetary value of the ring wasn't significant compared to the sentimental value. I felt as if I had betrayed her.

Things were a mess. I'm surprised the copper wasn't ripped out of my air conditioning unit and sold for scrap metal.

In the mornings, I woke up, grabbed my dog, and went to McDonald's for a large cup of coffee. I had a coffee maker at home, but it seemed too complicated and overwhelming to brew a pot of coffee. I didn't trust myself because the simplest tasks seemed monumental.

Every morning, I read devotionals and recovery materials for an hour. Looking back, that was precious time spent with God. I had no one making any demands on my time or energy, so I started to clean up my house. It was just me—room by room, closet by closet. I don't remember how long it took, but I was proud when it was done. It was a cleansing purge.

I tossed things of my grandmother's I had been holding onto for years. I dumped my ex's stuff, which was still lying around. I was sick of my surroundings reflecting other people. I wanted it to reflect me. It dawned on me I had a chance most people would never have. I could reinvent myself from scratch. I was beginning with a blank slate.

My mother was coming to visit soon, and I was excited about having company. My aunt traveled with her in case she needed backup and support. She was afraid I would not stay clean and would act crazy, which was understandable. I did not have a successful track record, all she had was her hope. After all, statistics are pretty grim for a woman my age trying to stay sober.

During her visit, my mother made me feel safe and helped me believe I could stay sober this time. My aunt left after a few days because she was bored. I still didn't have a TV, and I wasn't in a position to entertain. It was a good thing my mother likes to crochet and do crafts. She was very patient with me. She wanted me to move to Texas, but I wasn't ready for that.

I had ghosts to face where I lived, and I wasn't quite prepared for that either. I had done a lot of damage to others during my using, and a lot of damage was done to me. I knew I had to deal with it. And I would—in time.

While I wasn't ready to move to Texas, I realized an extended visit would be wonderful. I got permission from my probation officer for an extended visit and traveled to the Lone Star State with Mom. I thought my probation officer must have been amused when I brought my mommy to my first appointment. After all, I was fifty-three years old.

She and my stepfather took great care of me. They treated me like I was special and had achieved significant success. They viewed me through their unique lens of unconditional love.

If I could only begin to view myself that way.

In Texas, I was diligent about my recovery program. I attended two AA meetings daily, one at noon and the other at 7:00 p.m. I fell in love with a small community church and attended regularly. I made friends and started to get comfortable. Then it was time to go back; probation appointment was in a few days. My dog, Marty, and I made the road trip back to Florida. I had a new TV and was comfortable making a pot of coffee in the morning. Hey, for me, that was progress.

The couple that did the Bible study in rehab invited me to church with them. They went out of their way to pick me up on Sundays. When the worship music started, I could not hold back my tears. I stopped crying when the sermon started but could not stop during worship songs. I figured they were cleansing, healing tears. Just like cleaning my home, my heart and soul were being cleansed. My pain was being transformed. It became of the utmost importance to me that I be baptized. The Bible study lady set it up for me, and I was thrilled. I had a church community and a recovery community at home. One step at a time, one day at a time, I was getting healthier.

I carried guilt and self-loathing about my previous behaviors. I had changed, but who was going to believe that? I was on my way to face my ex while I spoke to my mother on the phone. I told her what I was about to do and shared that I felt scared and nervous. She said I would be fine and told me she trusted me. The idea of her trusting me shook me up. I realized no one could trust me when it came to drugs and alcohol. I especially could not trust myself. The trust she spoke of felt like too much pressure. She was sincere, but it was misplaced trust. At that moment, I knew that trusting God was going to be the only way I could stay sober. I told her not to trust me but to trust God. Another aha moment. I could not yet handle the burden of trust. Jeez, I had just started making coffee.

I secretly hoped to reunite with my ex. My fantasy was he would forgive me, profess his undying love for me, and we would live happily ever after. He was not on the same page. He was not open to getting back together at all, but I was not giving up, not yet. We had eviscerated each other. The hurt was still too fresh. I had to accept that or go crazy. Acceptance came, and I let go of my desire to have my way right now. I decided to have faith and believe if we were meant to be together, it would be in the future, and God would work it out. I never had a healthy relationship with a man and knew I had substantial growing and healing to do before I was ready. I had to learn to love myself. How could I learn to connect to the spirit I knew as

God and see myself the way people told me that He sees me? How could I get the trust from my head to my heart?

Estes Park: Here's Johnny!

Life was going well, but of course, there were obstacles that I called speed bumps. One of the larger obstacles was my ex because I still carried a torch for him. I stalked him into a parking lot at a gas station and got high afterward because poor me did not get my way. I had a complete screw-it moment and drove to the hood for some dope. I spent three hundred dollars that night on garbage dope and never got high. The next day, a friend came and took me to their house, so I wasn't alone with my thoughts. I was ripe for a relapse and furious with myself. The difference was, instead of keeping a huge secret and lying about it, I admitted it to my sponsor. That made it a mistake and not the end of the world. I could not keep one foot in a sober world and the other foot close to the abyss. Both feet had to be firmly planted in sobriety so my roots would grow deep and strong. After that, I got drunk one more time and hated the feeling. Amazingly, I no longer wanted to chase the feeling of oblivion. Aha, a pivotal moment! My new prayer became, "God, please do for me what I cannot do for myself. Please keep me sober today."

The experiences I had, and the things I learned, started to come together and make sense. There was a moment when God and I had a standoff. I had done everything I was told to do to stave off a craving to use, but I was giving in. I went for a ride to change my atmosphere, but my car automatically drove to the hood. Oh no, not this time. I pounded my fists on the steering wheel and said out loud, "God, you promised. Now do what you said you would. Please stop me from doing this!" I was more demanding than polite. I wanted Him to prove to me He was real. I was hungry, so I turned left into a pizza parlor. I heard worship music playing and saw a picture of Jesus on the wall as soon as I opened the door. I laughed so hard that I cried. He showed up big time. Okay, Okay, I get it. My trust and faith in this elusive God started to get very personal. I wondered where I was going from here.

I missed my family and wanted to plan a visit. I wanted to express my gratitude and thank them for all they did during my incarceration and rehab. I had not seen my sisters for a long time, and they were always a huge part of my life. The last time had been at my grandmother's funeral, and I was a mess. Mom's birthday was coming up, and we had planned a trip to Estes Park, Colorado. It was a reunion and a celebration. I was over the moon with excitement.

KELLY SPEAKS

I was elated to hear Karen was sober but have to admit I was somewhat skeptical. My attitude was "trust but verify." I had many conflicting emotions. I was anxious and excited to see her and spend quality time with her. I was still angry at her for all of the chaos and pain she had caused me. She had lied to me countless times. She had abandoned me and destroyed any semblance of a sister bond we shared in the past. I was fearful that the destruction and debris her addiction caused me would be beyond repair.

During the trip, I was waiting for Karen to express a sincere, detailed amends. My expectation was that Karen owed me a *big* amends. I know she believed there was nothing she could possibly say to heal the hurt she caused me. I realized that Karen had no memory of many of the incidents I was holding onto. There are times when it is not possible for a person to make a direct amends.

Our reunion became an opportunity for me to show forgiveness and kindness. Nothing could erase or fix the pain of the past, but our family desired to move into the future with a clean slate for each of us. Karen and I have learned that the best gift a person in recovery can give to their family is staying sober, which is a living amends. The prayers of our family had been answered.

KAREN SPEAKS

We stayed at the historic Stanley Hotel where we thought Stephen King's movie, *The Shining*, was filmed. Of course, we had all seen the movie. It was a classic. My youngest sister, Kolleen, wanted desperately to visit the maze where the movie's final scene occurred. At check-in, she asked the clerk where the maze was. He told her that the scene was shot in London and there was no maze at the hotel. He laughed and said everybody asks about the maze. Kolleen's face dropped, and she looked like she was going to cry. The joke was on us, I guess. Afterward, we all had a good laugh. We booked a junior suite in the main hotel area. The lobby was wonderfully appointed with beautiful antiques and other period pieces.

The "junior suite" was the size of a shoebox. We were four full-grown women sharing one tiny hotel room with a queen-size bed and a full-size pullout couch. We could barely walk around the furniture to get to the bathroom. There was no air-conditioning given the age of the hotel and location in the mountains. We did have a window, though, located right above the restaurant. The smoke from the wood-burning grill stunk up the room. It was ninety-three degrees in July, and this was unusually hot for the high elevation in the Rocky Mountains.

We did not care; we were three menopausal sisters getting hot flashes while vacationing with their mother. Air-conditioning was as crucial as oxygen itself for us. Everything seemed funny on this trip. The laughter and joy I experienced is indelibly branded in my brain. I felt so alive. Being immersed in nothing but love was incredible. I had let my guard down. I felt the love from my mother and sisters radiate out toward me. I hoped I reflected it back to them. We were all so happy to be together with no elephants in the room.

My sister, Kelly, the official vacation coordinator, got us upgraded to a two-bedroom, two-bath chalet for free. The girl is good. It had serious air-conditioning. We went on the ghost tour and had pictures of the ghosts to prove it. We ate mediocre food at a fancy, expensive restaurant in the Stanley Lodge and went on a bus tour of Estes Park. We found out that altitude sickness is a real thing as we were flatlanders.

It was surreal to me. I felt like I was in some other universe. Then it dawned on me; this is what a relaxed and sober life must be like. I got so excited. If this is what I have to look forward to—wow! —maybe I can keep it up.

My sisters stepped up big-time for me when I was in jail and treatment. They communicated with my attorney, and they took care of my bills and business. Thanking them and my mother seemed hollow and empty to me. "I'm sorry" became a cheap, meaningless statement. I never followed it up by genuinely changing. I knew the only way to make amends to my family was to live differently. This vacation gave me great motivation to do that. I remembered what it felt like to be this close to them.

Kelly and I have chosen a path to live sober lives and therefore share a special bond. I am so grateful for that. Alcoholism and addiction are hard for people to understand unless you have it. People will always say they don't understand why you can't stop after a few drinks, and we say we don't understand how you can. What the recovery process does is get rid of crippling shame and guilt.

I found out recovery doesn't happen by magic; it is like a recipe. If I put in the right ingredients, the cake will be great. How simple is that? It seems like common sense. Well, it is. Trust God + make good choices = a great life. Trust yourself + make shady choices = not so great a life. This simple recipe is the hardest thing I have ever made. Like everything else, the more I practice fundamental principles, the more automatic it becomes. I don't have to think about how to brush my teeth. I just do it—every day since I was a little girl. Once I was taught how, I had to stay vigilant and brush them daily.

It is the same with staying sober for me. I must remain vigilant. A sober life feels like freshly brushed teeth to me. I want to be clear I made none of these changes alone. Thinking I could figure it out myself held me back for many years. I found out that a doctor could not cure a spiritual blockage, neither could a therapist, hypnotist, shrink, snake-oil salesman, nor the multitude of other equations I tried over the years. No one else could do the work for me. If I could have bought my recovery off a shelf in a store, I would have. If I could have paid someone to do it for me, I would have. I would have appreciated the ease and comfort of little effort for maximum results. The reward for doing the hard stuff comes when you reach the other side. I had a gut feeling I wasn't quite there yet.

I got past a few speed bumps and had eighteen months of sobriety. I was deeply committed to this path. I was happy with the life I was building. My ex was still not interested in seeing me or even having lunch together. Since I believed that was a dead end, I started to date someone. How weird that was. It felt like a hundred years since I had been on a date. A few dates later, I knew I was far from ready for anything other than a friendship with a man. Relationships were way too complicated for me, and I enjoyed hanging out with the girls. After a few months, my new friend left and went back up north. Great, no one got hurt or scarred.

I requested my ex come and get the few things he left at the house, or I threatened I'd throw them away. I was still using manipulative tactics. I don't know why I could not be honest with him and ask him to talk. An honest and healthy relationship was an anomaly to me. He came over to pick his things up and politely let me know he had started seeing someone.

Another throat punch. I was sick to my stomach. I suddenly felt like all the hard work I had done was not worth it. I thought about getting high, but I did not. I realized the hard work was worth it because I did it for myself this time and no one else. I might go off the deep end emotionally, but I would not let this be an excuse to get high.

It seemed like all my anger, fear and insecurity started to bubble up through my body. I began to cry and shake uncontrollably and could not stop. I felt like my deepest fear was coming true. I was going to be stuck in a state of despair with no way out. I believed I was doomed. I had to find a way to stop shaking and crying, so I drove to the emergency room. I went through the triage process and saw a doctor.

When he asked me what was so horrible, I realized my answer would sound ridiculous. I would look like a complete idiot if I said, "Oh, my boyfriend, who I have been separated from for three years, is dating someone else." Are you kidding? So, I made something up.

He gave me a valium and told me to see a shrink. Then I got a bill for nine hundred dollars in the mail. The doctor never even listened to my heart with a stethoscope.

Well, psychotherapy was out of the question. So, at this point, it was between God and me. I cried to my sponsor and a few friends, and no one understood the problem because my boyfriend and I had broken up a long time ago. I did not even comprehend my severe reaction and knew it was out of proportion to the circumstance.

My mom and stepdad were my safe haven, so off to Texas I went. I knew this breakdown of sorts was a big hurdle. If I could get through this without picking up a drink or drug, I had gotten to the other side. The emotions I avoided and squashed throughout my life were coming out like a raging river. My previous coping mechanisms of alcohol and drugs were no longer an option. I stayed in Texas for a month, hoping my angst would magically disappear.

It did not, but I had garnered enough strength to go home and deal with my life. I was determined. I was doing childish things like showing up at the same meetings my ex went to and staring laser beams at his head. I wanted him to be uncomfortable. If I wrote the things I wanted to do to him and his girlfriend, I would be back in the Nut House. They had become the target and focal point of my vitriol. I tried to use the skills I learned in the past eighteen months, but it was not working.

I was in enough emotional pain that I gave in and sought extra help. There was only one doctor in the world that I believed in and trusted, William Leach, MD. I knew he had his patients' best interest at heart. Dr. Leach is an addiction specialist I met years before. He helped me medically detox from opiates without needing hospitalization. He was the real deal, and I called him a healer. This man went out of his way for addicts, and for this I respected him a great deal. I was intrigued by him and a bit smitten. He shared some fascinating experiences, like his spiritual quest to India. He owned his own plane and had exotic travel adventures. I knew I could count on him since he always answered my calls, day or night.

At first, I was adamantly opposed to any psychiatric medications, although that was his recommendation. I was afraid I would go back to using if I could not stop shaking and learn to relax, so I reluctantly agreed.

He told me if I had not picked up yet, he did not think I would. I clung to that. After all, he was a doctor. In addition, he asked me what I believed was the most important thing I learned in rehab. I responded, "I know I'm I not worthless." He smiled and told me I was cured. That was the first time I'd laughed and felt positive in months. I also agreed to see a therapist. Who, me? The one who pooh-poohs all shrinks and therapy? Yes, that's right; I decided to give it a shot with an open mind and an open heart.

I prayed about my state of mind and asked God to show me what was inside of me that made me react like this. What was revealed to me was a memory from childhood.

When I was a child, I saw things and knew things but was absolutely powerless over them. On some level I understood that my father was not faithful to my mother. He did not try hard to hide it. I remembered a party that my grandparents had at their summer bungalow. My sisters and I were there as well as my mom. Dad got drunk and was making out with this girl in plain sight. He did not care if his wife or kids saw him. Everyone saw him. I felt my mother's pain and humiliation. She stayed with him through years of abuse. He was a violent drunk.

Growing up like that is like living with a terrorist. You are never sure when the bomb will drop, so you are always hyper-alert. I was tense and insecure my whole life. I never felt safe. I had the mistaken belief that the long-standing relationship with my boyfriend provided me with security. When I thought that was over, it rocked my foundation of life. It was just another lie I believed. If I could not trust myself or other people to keep me safe, who could I trust?

I understood there was a new foundation for my life. A real one. A source of security, love, wisdom, justice, and strength that would never run out as long as I stayed plugged in. This source is available for everyone and is known by many names. I know him as God. My journey to find Him had been long and arduous. I knew He was the only way to heal this awful pain. I was no longer resigned to my life of circumstances.

Again, I relinquished myself into the hands of my heavenly Father. My prayer was answered. He reached in and pulled the root of my pain out; it could not grow back because the source was dead. Over the next few months, I found a joy to be unequaled. My body stopped shaking internally and externally. I was able to stop taking all meds except an antidepressant. I don't even think I need that because I am probably one of the happiest people you would ever meet, but I now follow my doctor's directions. Taking instruction from experts is a new part of my personality.

Every day became exciting for me. I had no particular goal in life; I was just grateful to have a life. My gratitude deepens continuously. I am convinced that gratitude is the key to peace and happiness. It is a quiet, calm internal peace that has nothing to do with any circumstance or happening. It is the grace of God.

My healing started to feel real and, dare I say, permanent. I was no longer afraid of myself. I began to trust my choices and decisions. Emotional and spiritual growth began at an exponential pace. I have seen people in the recovery rooms over the years that profess long-term sobriety. To me, many still seemed outright miserable. If that were my sobriety, I would just as soon drink, but who am I to judge? If it works for them, great. I am sure they pass on wisdom and experience to people who need to hear what they have to say. We are all valuable. Everyone has a story to share. I found out that I did not have the corner on pain. My pain was not unique. I was no better or worse than anyone; I just was.

The most exceptional people have come into my life. Of course, I mean my family first. Without them and their support, I would not be this new version of me. I have a mentor that I met at church whom I adore. We study and learn together and discover amazing things about God and His world. We have a deep appreciation and love for each other.

One of the most significant differences between the old me and the new me is I am capable of forming and sustaining meaningful relationships. I have real friends, and I am a real friend to others. Not an acquaintance or a party buddy. I don't have to lie about who I am or hide it. I am comfortable in my own skin, and I'm not ashamed to be me.

I have learned to live in the present. I do not worry about the future; I choose to trust God with it.

Above all, I have been forgiven for the past. I have also forgiven myself. Now that I know there is a better way of life, I am responsible for living it. I am also responsible for passing it on. How can I do that?

Fun in sobriety: Kelly's tandem skydiving jump to celebrate her fiftieth birthday.

The dreaded haunted room #217 at the Stanley Hotel in Estes Park during our family vacation July 2014. Karen was out of rehab and sober.

Karen's graduation and completion of her minister's license, July 20, 2017.

Mom and Karen relaxing on the grounds of the Stanley Hotel.

Family restored: Jerry, Mom, Karen, Kendra, Kollen, Kelly.

20

From Darkness into Light

KELLY SPEAKS

Being in recovery and living a sober lifestyle has been the most significant gift in my life. It's been so meaningful and powerful, it's hard for me to express in words. Admitting my alcoholism was devastating. I had accumulated so much guilt, shame, and humiliation. *Alcohol was a good friend to me. A friend I could count on to calm me down, never talk back, and was always available to me. I grieved losing it.* This may sound bizarre but true.

The five stages of grief are denial, anger, bargaining, depression, and acceptance. Of course, these stages are not wrapped up in a nice, neat little bow. I fluctuated back and forth among them for years and, at times, still do. I knew the stages of denial and bargaining well and shifted between both for years before getting sober. How could I be grieving for a thing, an inanimate object? Anger was my go-to defense when I was hurt by someone or fearful of a situation, which was often.

Learning to live a sober lifestyle meant that I would have to walk through all I had been avoiding, consciously or unconsciously—all of my sorrows I had been drowning in the bottle. In early sobriety, depression hit. The most routine daily tasks seemed overwhelming. While drinking, my world got increasingly secretive and isolated. I felt more alone and despondent because I knew I couldn't keep my current lifestyle, friends, activities, and routine if I wanted to stay sober. I was broken. I asked myself, "What did I have to lose?" I became willing to do what was suggested to me by others living successful, sober lives. My recovery is an ongoing process.

I learned that recovery is for people who want it; it's not for people who need it. This is an unfortunate truth. The outcome for those people who need recovery but don't want it is grim. Those with active addiction eventually end up part of a tragedy that leads to jail or death. Their loved ones are left behind to manage the wreckage and pain of what seems like a senseless loss.

Do not end up a statistic. We are not numbers. Our lives matter. If you or a loved one has a problem with alcohol or drugs, don't give up.

Keep seeking, and you will find a solution. There are many paths to the same destination.

Freedom awaits!

For me, recovery was an inside job. I had faith. Not necessarily the faith defined in religious doctrines. My definition of faith was believing in something I could not see, feel, or touch. As I talk about my spiritual belief and practice, I'm not talking about organized religion. We all carry experiences from our upbringing and our parents' belief systems into adulthood. I enjoyed and benefited from the rituals and ceremonies of organized religion. I also experienced the limitations and hypocrisy. I believe religious organizations and institutions are man-made and therefore inherently fallible. These institutions are multitrillion dollar businesses.

That said, I do attend church. I like to sing and worship and show my gratitude to my higher power, who is God. As I speak about God,

I'm talking about a direct connection to Him, not through a priest, minister, or any other representative. I'm talking about physics, a universal life force, or universal consciousness—for those of you who are atheists or agnostics. To me, a higher power is something undefinable and much greater than we can fathom.

I began to practice faith. I didn't know a damn thing about how to live sober, but fortunately, other people did. For me, the 12-step program of Alcoholics Anonymous was the vessel that showed me the way. The twelve steps are simple in concept but not easy to implement.

I hope the reader can put aside any preconceived notions or stereotypes. Purchase a copy of the *Big Book* and read it. It's a compelling novel, even if you don't have an alcohol problem. I hope you will enjoy it!

Early on, I was told to get on my knees and pray to stay sober for a twenty-four-hour period. I thought it was stupid but took the action anyway. I prayed to God, but you can pray to your own higher power. I prayed to God to please lift my obsessive thoughts about alcohol and my desire to drink. I remember within thirty days, my prayer came true. What a relief! Because those thoughts were all-consuming and occupied a large portion of my daily energy and brain!

The slogans of AA (found in aa.org) are full of contradictions.

Surrender to win. How does surrendering and waving the white flag bring freedom?

Let go, let God. I was taught not to depend on others. My dad told me to be tough and maintain my independence no matter what. I'm not going to review the twelve steps or the AA program, but I love AA's slogans.

Here are some of my favorites, although thoroughly reviewing these slogans could be a novel in and of itself.

I can't. He can. I'll let Him. My way wasn't working, so why not try something different? Here is the thing, *I had to ask. I had to ask* *for help.* I was fiercely independent and had to admit to myself that I couldn't get sober alone.

We will love you until you learn to love yourself. I thought it was so corny when the women in AA said this, and I wanted to gag. Now, I'm eternally grateful, and I have friends for a lifetime I know I can count on. I know I will never be alone.

Today, I look into the mirror and like the reflection I see looking back. I don't seek outside validation anymore because I have learned that I'm a child of God and worthy of everything good. It is a relief to turn my fears over to a higher power and know I can let them go. The past is a trail I've blazed; there is no going back. I can't change it. What I can do is work toward being the best version of myself. I'm empowered to create my new truths.

Pause when agitated or doubtful. We are a culture of now. Access to technology has made us more impatient than ever. We expect immediate responses to texts. This led me to intolerance, impatience, and knee-jerk reactions. I've learned to pause and take time to evaluate what has upset me. It is incredible what avoiding an immediate response can do to a situation. We have all heard, "Well, let me sleep on it." This works! I've realized that I don't need to respond to someone immediately. Frankly, it's not a realistic expectation for anyone to think that they have access to another person twenty-four seven. The recipient deserves a thoughtful and kind response.

Here's an example. I told one of my sisters that I would not help my dad financially when he moved from Grenada to Texas. Within twenty-four hours, she texted me and asked me to cosign a rental agreement for my father. I couldn't believe she completely disregarded our conversation. My initial reaction was to blast her back a condescending text asking her what part of our conversation did she not hear or understand. Instead, I decided not to respond at all.

The next day, the situation was resolved. Choosing not to respond was a more powerful message than confronting her directly.

Another time, one of my nephews sent me a lengthy text asking if he could come visit with Bob and me for a while. He was over twenty-one and having conflict with his parents. He pledged to follow my house rules, which included no smoking cigarettes or marijuana, no drinking, gaining employment, and completing chores. He assured me he would be the perfect house guest.

After that text, I learned that his drinking was causing havoc in his relationships and employment. I was not willing to invite this type of chaos into my home.

I texted him back and asked him to call me directly to talk further. I told him he was always welcome. My criteria for him to stay with us would be demonstrating ninety days of sobriety. He would have to complete UAs and show abstinence from drugs or alcohol before visiting.

This quickly ended the conversation and the request. I didn't want to have this discussion via text messaging. I felt it was essential to have a dialogue and to keep the door open for the future.

E-mails and texts are often a form of one-way communication and notification. It's not a way to have a meaningful exchange. I guess I'm old school when it comes to this. I did pause in this situation because I didn't want to be punitive with my nephew and wasn't sure how to address his request in a way that would allow me to be clear about my limits and give him the message that he was loved.

Live and let live. This slogan suggests that I should accept how other people live and behave, especially if they do things differently than me. It requires tolerance. It means I must evaluate my judgment, expectations, and need to control others.

I'm in recovery, and I AM an alcoholic, but at times I still scratch my head and question why someone would do the things they do under the influence of alcohol or drugs. It looks self-destructive, and it is. I can imagine how insane these behaviors seem to a typical drinker.

Every person has the right to blaze their trail even when it leads to death. I don't have the right to judge someone else's choices or behaviors—what a relief! Control is an illusion. I tried for years to control my drinking and Karen's drug addiction. I thought I knew what was best for her. I wanted her to conform to my timetable and do what I wanted her to do when I wanted her to do it.

It was only when I truly let go and realized that I didn't have the answer that I gained some sanity. I was able to let go of the outcome and accept whatever the future would bring. God's plan was much more than I could have ever imagined!

Progress over perfection. Today I've learned to show kindness and compassion to myself. I freely demonstrated these virtues toward others in the past but now have learned to extend the same gentleness to myself. I've stopped seeking perfection for it is an illusion.

All of my life, I sought to be at the top. I identified as a Type A personality and wore this label with pride. I'm known to be highly competitive in sports and even board games.

However, trying to be perfect is a no-win situation. I was performing for recognition as a way to mask my insecurities and perceived shortcomings. There is nothing wrong with setting achievable goals. Goals are important. Presently, I won't allow a relative or friend to impose their expectations for performance on me. Instead, I will do my best and be present in my interactions with others. The most significant gift I can give others is my time and attention. I work toward being present in my relationships. All I ever wanted in my family was to be seen and heard. I wanted to have a voice. Today, I do. Also, hugs, smiles, and genuine compliments are free. Give abundantly!

Happy, Joyous, and Free at Last

KAREN SPEAKS

Maintenance of a lifestyle is ongoing and conscious. If something or someone is ignored or forgotten, they will wither away like an unkempt garden. Now, my purpose in life is simple. If I see someone or something withering, I water it. I do that in many different ways. I am no savior, but I try to emulate my heavenly Savior.

I have a nickname for myself. It is the "opposite girl." To change everything is not as hard as it sounds. The two things that must change for that to happen is your thinking and your mind. I found out I could not change that on my own. I tried and failed miserably.

Once I truly opened my mind and heart, life seemed to change in spite of me. I no longer wanted to be rebellious and anti-everything. I found a tremendous amount of wisdom in the restraint of pen and tongue.

The abyss in my heart grew and grew until I believed it to be fatal. Nothing outside of me would fill it anymore. I tried in every way possible to fill it. Finally, I gave up, and in giving up, I struck an infinite source. I am tapped into God's power. To stay connected, it must flow through me.

I do not have a list of things I do for others or a minimum amount of good deeds to do daily. I trust that God will show me when it is my turn to help. My story is not unique. There are tons of women in jail and prison for lesser things than I have done. I am compelled by the love that has been so freely given to me, to share with all women, that it is available to them. To watch the light in another person's eyes shine with the revelation of God's love is the most significant reward of my sobriety. To watch someone else recover and be a part of that is the most incredible honor I have experienced. I am blessed with that honor.

I am one of over seven billion people on the planet. I have it better than some and not as good as others. I would no longer trade my life for anything. In meetings, I heard people say they had a life second to none. I thought that was bogus because their lives didn't look so great from where I was sitting. I am sure it is the same when people look at my life now. I am sixty years old, and a good chunk of my time has passed. I am retired, so my major productive years are considered over. I can pay my bills, but I'm far from monetarily rich. I am twenty pounds over-weight, which I have accepted because I love cake. I also love myself, just like I am. That is why I consider my life second to none. I am rich with new mercy every morning—for myself and others.

My fantasy for the whole world is to find this source of joy for themselves. If I could, I would give it to everyone. It is available to everyone. It is a gift. It is grace. You don't have to buy it, and you cannot earn it. You just have to ask God for it by opening your heart and mind and then be willing. The rest, God will take care of.

Afterword

Neither one of us would have voluntarily chosen the paths we walked, especially the abuse we suffered as children. Our lives have been roller-coaster rides with steep inclines and descents, unexpected sharp curves, and sudden changes of speed.

As we reflect on our journeys, we can see how our hardships and pain have been healed and then used for a larger purpose. We value our sobriety and face life one day at a time. We are eternally grateful for the unbreakable bond we have with our family; it's a bond that has been a consistent thread through all our ups and downs.

And we thank you, dear reader, now forever part of our hearts.

Acknowledgements

KELLY

I want to express my gratitude and thanks to the fellowship of Alcoholics Anonymous and the women of my home group. You know who you are! Thank you for the hugs, shared tears, openness, and support you have given to me over the last sixteen years.

Thank you to Fran Gallaher and Really Flourish, who, while we were brainstorming over lunch, gave me the idea for the book. Immediately, I knew it was the story I had to write.

I'm eternally grateful to Patty Evans, who was my boss, mentor, and later a trusted friend. When I reached out asking for help, she responded with genuine care and concern. She directed me to the resources I needed to start my recovery.

Thank you to Lola Heckman, who has been with me every step of the way. She is my confidant, friend, and sponsor and has shown me what true unconditional love is.

Thank you to Karen, my oldest sister, who jumped in with both feet and enthusiastically said yes when I asked her to write this memoir with me. It's been such a joyful and healing experience for the both of us.

Most importantly, thank you to my husband, Robert Ryan, who supported me from the beginning of the project, encouraged me when I was discouraged, and is my greatest fan. He is a gift from God and my best friend.

KAREN

I would like to thank my Lord and Savior, Jesus Christ, who changed my life into one worth living. I'm grateful to the women at Project Warm Rehab, who selflessly gave of themselves to show complete strangers a new way of living. Also, my very wise women friends from my AA groups who knew me better than I knew myself.

Thank you to First Assembly Church of DeLand, Florida, for being a real community church and spreading love around our town. I met my best friend and mentor, Dottie Tasker, at this church, and we keep learning together.

I want to thank my soul sister/twin sister, Kelly, who opened her heart back up to me after I had hurt her so deeply. The time spent doing this project with you has been a wonderful and rich bonding experience.

Lastly, thank you to Robert Larkin Junior, my partner in life. I love you with all of my heart and can't imagine doing life without you!

Both of Us

We are so appreciative to Karen Eusebio and our sister, Kolleen Bailey, who read the manuscript multiple times to help us edit and encouraged us to stay vulnerable and honest. We enjoyed the laughter, tears, and conversations that were generated by this experience. We are so grateful to Karen Scalf Bouchard, our book coach, who helped us take a rough draft and turn it into this heartwarming and beautiful story.

We must recognize our parents, Rosemarie and Jerry Hinkle. Our mom has been our biggest fan and cheerleader throughout this process. Her love and encouragement is endless. Our stepdad, Jerry, has shown us what a father's love is. We are eternally grateful to him and the way that he demonstrates his love and affection to our family.

Thank you to Kendra Heintzelman, our other sister and my Irish twin. We are so grateful that Kendra and Kolleen have been with us every step of the way, and we are forever bonded as sisters and friends.

About the Authors

KELLY RYAN is a licensed marriage and family therapist who has spent over thirty years in the field of Special Education, mental health, substance abuse and Educational Consulting placement services, helping families, troubled adolescents and young adults. She enjoys the splendor of the outdoors and spending time in nature. Kelly is always open to new adventures and travel. She loves gardening, reading, and hiking. She's grateful to her family's endless support in all her endeavors and particularly as an author. She resides in Colorado with her husband of thirty-one years.

KAREN BURD spends most of her time giving back to the communities that have helped her along the way. She's active in a women's jail ministry, the local recovery community, and her church. She lives in DeLand, Florida, with her life partner, Bob, and their precious pug, Marty. She looks forward to spending time with her family, enjoys reading, walking on the beach, and spending time at the local dog park with Marty and his friends.